No Stone Unturned

No Stone Unturned

The Carl and Rosie Story

Rosemarie Stone

Ian Randle Publishers
Kingston • Miami

First published in Jamaica, 2007 by
Ian Randle Publishers
11 Cunningham Avenue
Box 686
Kingston 6
www.ianrandlepublishers.com

© 2007, Rosemarie Stone

National Library of Jamaica Cataloguing in Publication Data

Stone, Rosemarie
    No stone unturned : the Carl and Rosie story / Rosemarie Stone.

        p. ;   cm.

    ISBN 978-976-637-308-5 (pbk)

1. Stone, Carl – 1940-1993 - Biography.   2. Stone, Rosemarie - Biography.
3. Biography - Jamaica.   4. AIDS (Disease) - Jamaica.
I. Title

    920   dc 22

Cover and book design by Ian Randle Publishers
Printed in the United States of America

DEDICATION

This book is dedicated to my sister Andrea for all the loving things she has done for me; they are too numerous to mention. Thank you, especially, for physically looking after and protecting me when I was ill. You are an integral part of everything that I write – I enjoyed the difficult and cathartic process we shared together in putting the events that are contained in this manuscript on paper. I am grateful for your typing skills, and your determined effort in finding the perfect proverbs.

TABLE OF CONTENTS

ACKNOWLEDGEMENTS

To Tricia and Timothy, my children, and Chloe my granddaughter; without you this journey would be incomplete and unnecessary.

To my father Darrell – thanks for believing that I would complete this project.

To all my siblings – Shirley, Mark, June, Barry, Leslie, Rena and Andrea, for their continued love and for supporting me in all that I do. Also to their wives, husbands and partners for all that they do.

To all my relatives – you have all been a source of strength to me.

To Leroy, Carl's brother who provided the buffer between me and his family who didn't know and could not understand, hence were judgmental. To Susan, his wife – for caring.

To Marcia Lewis – thank you for taking care of me and my family.

To Dr Grace who did everything that was humanly and medically possible for Carl and me.

To Dr Barry whom I called every night at a quarter to twelve to share the burdens of my day during the period 1992–1993.

To Dr Matt who provided counselling and hugs in his office that I dubbed the 'crying room'.

To Dr Steinhart and his staff, thank you for creating a safe, welcoming environment where I felt like a human being and could begin the process of healing physically and mentally. Special thanks to Elsa for all your kindness and help.

To all my friends who provided me with emotional, physical, financial and social support; thanks for all the telephone calls, cards and letters. Some of you read the manuscript and were pleased. Some of you provided professional services free of cost. Carmen Cameron, Carol Lawes, Carol Narcisse, Carol and Wayne Wong, Cecile Phillip, Claire Osbourne, Cliff and Joan Stone, Deidra James, Derryck Mamby, Donna Stephenson, Earl Mckenzie, Gail and George Wilson, George and Janet Phillip, Gracie Edwards, Harold Brady, Howard and Charmaine Gregory, Hyacinth Simmonds, Janice Wright, Jennifer Fray, John Ulett, Lana and Royden Riettie, Lloyd and Winnie Hunter, Marlene Rickets, Marlene and Errol Kennedy, Maureen and 'Flash' Williams, Mauvette and Keith Wedderburn, Merris and Errol Maye, Nicky Bragg, Noreen Beadle, Norma Spence, Pansie Bernkopef, Pansy Brown, Pansy and Hindley Williams, Peter and Janice Chang, Sharon and Steve Shelton, Shelly and Peter Glaze, Yasmin Williams, Valarie and Dennis Thompson, Vallie and Keith Reynolds, Wanda Harris, Winston and Sonia Davidson.

To Father Anthony Palazzaolo who is the one priest who can claim that I truly love him; who helped me to deal with a lot of the by products of HIV. I especially thank him for the part he played in dealing with my femininity and womanhood. He inspired me to write, without him this book would not exist.

To Suzanne Beadle, my cousin and in-house editor, who worked tirelessly with me to put this manuscript together.

To Ian Randle, my publisher, who believed in the book on first reading.

PROLOGUE:
YUH SPREAD YUH BED HARD,
YUH MUS HAV FE LIE HARD PON IT

If you make your bed and share it, when discomfort comes, you bear it

Dear Reader,

I invite you on this journey of exploration with me as I share the experiences in my life during a very difficult period: 1991–2006. My life before this I thought of as normal. I am the eldest of eight children, five girls and three boys, born to my father Darrell, an electrician, and my mother Winnifred, a housewife. Our large and loud household included me and my siblings, Shirley, Mark, June, Barry, Leslie, Rena and Andrea. I was born in Kingston, Jamaica on October 8, 1947 and the youngest, Andrea, in 1959 – eight of us over a 12-year period.

I had a contentious relationship with my father but my love of reading and movies, my interest in politics and world affairs and my love of all sports, especially cricket, derived from him. He influenced the child I was and the woman I became. He was not pleased to have a first daughter whom he thought was too friendly, laughed too easily with others and had a loud laugh that he termed 'raucous'. 'Rose,' he would say, 'a loud laugh shows a vacant mind.' As children are sometimes destined to do the opposite of what they are told by their parents, the older I grew the louder my laughter became and the more enjoyment I got from a good laugh. A friend once remarked, 'Don't let Rose laugh at you, because you will be well laughed at.'

For me, one of the perks of training to be a teacher and actually teaching in the classroom was that I got a chance to enter other people's lives that were sometimes completely different from mine. This was done either through interacting with children or their parents. This cultural diversity provided me with joyous memories. In 1969, at the end of my two-year in-house training course at Mandeville Teachers' College, we were assigned one-year internships at various schools across the island to complete our three-year training course. I had volunteered to do my internship at a 'closed school'. These schools were 'closed' because they did not have any teachers to man them. The Ministry of Education had devised a plan to open these schools using interns. Baxter's Mountain* in the parish of St. Mary, that appeared beside my name and the names of Valerie, Marjorie and Phyllis, my fellow interns, was somewhere that we had never heard of before and were unable to locate on the Jamaican map.

I loved everything about Baxter's Mountain – the long winding roads it took to get there, the remoteness and the isolation I felt once I was there. I cherished the memory of early mornings when the mist was dense and masked the lush vegetation until the sun peeped out slowly uncovering the surrounding hills that seemed

*For additional information on Baxter's Mountain, see appendix iii

to display several hues of green. I appreciated the river that played such a vital role in our lives and in the districts surrounding Baxter's Mountain. It provided Baxter's Mountain with a pathway to everywhere else. When this river was in 'spate', overflowed its banks, I was in awe of its power and the control it had to bring life to a standstill. There were many times when Valerie and I, after returning from a weekend in Kingston, found ourselves sitting on some huge stones by the river, waiting for hours, until the water receded and it was safe enough so that we could take off our shoes and cross the river to open the school for that Monday.

During this internship year, Valerie and I attended a funeral service for a young father who died. This was my first funeral at Pleasant Hill, a village across the river where quite a few students who attended Baxter's Mountain Primary School lived. The service was not conducted in a church but close to the gravesite. Amid cries of 'Teacher, mi cyaan believe him ded' was the interplay of grief, singing and the drinking of alcohol, which were all amazing to me.

The preacher's words were even more amazing. It seemed to me that he was actually quarrelling with the dead and saying words to the living that were hurtful rather than comforting. To compound my astonishment, the grieving family and friends all said 'Amen' to every statement he made. One such statement was, 'Dease young people of today, dem greedy, dem tell lie, dem drink, dem kill each other, dem covet wat don't belong to dem, dem fornicate and when dem can't do betta, dem dead.' There was an immediate rousing 'Amen' and I felt inappropriate laughter bubbling inside me as

Valerie came closer and whispered, 'We have to control ourselves.'

I saw acquiring a teacher's diploma as the first rung on the ladder of my independence. While I was at teachers' college, I fell in love and had my first serious relationship at the age of 21. This 'first love' was an, on again, off again romance for the next five years of my life and never really ended for me until the day I realized that I was getting involved with Carl Stone. During this six year period, 1968–1974, I enjoyed dating, sometimes in groups, and developed relationships that would become lifelong friendships. When I met Carl, having a relationship with him, platonic or otherwise, was not on the agenda, so falling passionately in love with, and getting married to him was not part of the plan I had envisioned for myself. Carl finally persuaded me to marry him and the date was set for July 5, 1975. All the invitations were sent out. After a very argument-driven meeting between my parents' pastor, Carl and myself, my mother wanted to have a talk with me. I did not particularly want to have this talk because it had become clear to me that my family was getting increasingly sceptical about me marrying Carl.

'Rose I am really surprised at you.'
'Why Momma, because Carl and I argued with your pastor?'
'No, I am surprised that you want to get married to somebody who has been married more than once.'
'Where did you hear that from?'

'It does not matter where I heard that from, the fact is that you did not tell us that Carl was married before.'
'I didn't think that it was anybody else's business but Carl's and mine. I am the one who is marrying Carl. He is not getting married to the whole family.'
'But Rose, you must have thought that it was something we would not like, that is why you kept it from us.'
'I am not thrilled to be marrying somebody who was married before, I am thrilled to be marrying Carl and I am going to marry him regardless of what you say.'
'I am really amazed at you Rose, because you always said you would not get married at all. And to choose someone who was married before, and from what I understand his marriages lasted for only a short time, is really out of character.'
'I did say that I did not want to get married. I am still unsure if I will be able to sustain a marriage. But I am in love with Carl and feel that we are compatible.'
'But Rose, suppose he leaves you like he left all the others?'
'Well, you, your pastor and the elders in your church who were quick to report information that didn't concern them, will be proved right, that's all.'
'Rose you shouldn't talk like that. They are concerned for you...'
'As a matter of fact Momma, you know me, I didn't want the kind of wedding that this has turned out to be with all those people…'
'Rose, are you speaking about my friends? I have only invited a few close ones.'
'Not only your friends, but I am speaking about family members too.'

'What do you mean Rose?'

'Since my marriage to Carl is causing so much confusion and heartache to you and other members of the family, I am going back to my original plan, plan A, a very small wedding with my circle of friends and persons who are on my side.'

'What are you saying Rose?'

'I am saying that July 5th is no longer my wedding date. All invitations for that date are null and void.'

'Don't you think that is a little extreme?'

'No, I feel joyful about being married to Carl and I do not want anybody at my wedding who does not share this view.'

'What about your friends?'

'Momma, I am very upset with you for speaking with my friends about this issue. If any of them has any misgivings, they will not be invited either.'

'Rose, you know that your friends all love you. They did not say anything negative about you or Carl.'

'They had better not.'

'Rose I want you to think about this very carefully. I know that in the past you have turned down three offers of marriage. . .'

'Please do not bring that up Momma, because you, more than anybody else, know that I did not consider accepting even one of those proposals. But now, after exploring my own misgivings about marriage I have accepted this proposal from Carl.'

'You can turn this one down too. There is still time to do so. I just want what is best for you. I am sorry your father is not here to speak to you on this matter.'

'Yes Momma, I know he will be home shortly and I

suspect that he will share your view on this subject and will completely take your side.'

Daddy was away at work. At this particular time he was working on a tugboat that remained at sea for sometimes up to three months. He was not at home when the breakdown of plans for my wedding day took place. When he got back I had already talked over the whole matter with Carl and we decided to get married by a marriage officer on the lawns of the house where he lived. I had also asked my sister June who lived in Chicago to print 20 new wedding invitations. The new wedding date was June 28, 1975.

To my surprise Daddy did not go along with the rest of the family. He thought that there was over-reaction to the details of the past and not enough consideration for the essential issue that I had fallen in love and wanted to get married. He said he trusted my judgement on questions related to Carl. This was the cue for my mother and the rest of the family to fall in line. I had the best, *my* wedding with about 20 people. I remember the evening now with great affection.

Carl and I travelled all over Jamaica for work and pleasure. We travelled together for polling and on occasions when he was invited to be a guest speaker or to take part in seminars anywhere from Negril to Morant Point; one end of the island to the other. The Bog Walk Gorge is a route that we used frequently when returning to Kingston from various parts of the country. The countryside of Jamaica is lush and beautiful. It is said historically that the gorge was formed when a limestone cave collapsed. As a result of this, the roadway was built between the Rio Cobre River on one side and the 'towering vertical walls of limestone'[1] on the other side. Flat bridge, built by the Spanish, is just a few feet above the water level of the Rio Cobre River. Heavy rains add to the drama of the gorge as it makes the bridge impassable and therefore the gorge inaccessible. Driving through the gorge's narrow, snaking road can be challenging and intimidating. This is even more daunting at dusk because the roadway is not well lit.

On one occasion while driving our VW through the Bog Walk Gorge, back from Ocho Rios late one Sunday evening, a pig crossed the road in front us seemingly out of nowhere and we hit it with the right side of our bumper. Immediately there was a new sound coming from the car. When Carl stopped the car to examine it, he found that the bumper was touching the tyre. He returned to the car to tell me what had happened. My laughter was full blown. I couldn't even respond to Carl. He kept on saying 'Rose, you have to control yourself, this is not a laughing matter.' We tried to drive the car a short distance but it became evident that something had to be done about the bumper in order for us to reach Kingston.

Carl had to use all his strength to pull the bumper from the tyre. He was concerned about getting the tyre damaged and having to change it. Each time we tried to drive the sound came back and my laughter

---

[1] Paul Zach, *Jamaica* (Singapore, Hong Kong: Apa Productions (HK) Ltd, 1983).

came along with it. He continued doing this several times until there was no more sound. When we could finally drive without interruption, Carl told me he was flabbergasted as to how I could laugh at what he thought could have been a serious situation.

'Rose, did you realize that there was a serious security risk? We are alone, in the dark, on the Bog Walk Gorge.'

'No man, not a thing was going to happen. But where do you think the pig came from?'

'Suppose I couldn't pull the bumper from the tyre?'

'It's a good thing you are such a strong man, but Carl, did you ever see a pig cross the street out of nowhere like that?'

'Rose, be serious.'

'Carl, not only the pig, but did you ever hear a car make a sound like that? I don't know which was stranger, the pig crossing the road or the sound of the car.'

When I married Carl, he thought my laughter one of my more attractive assets, although the timing of the mirth sometimes left him speechless. To be truthful my laughter was fuelled in part by Carl's response to the situation. Similar scenarios occurred many times during our marriage. It is some of the events of my marriage to Carl that I want to share with you.

Carl Stone was born in St. Elizabeth, Jamaica, in June 1940. He got his high school education from Wolmer's and Kingston College boys' schools. Before going to University, he was an Executive Officer in the Town Clerk's office at the KSAC. He got his BSc in

Government at the University of the West Indies in 1968. He went to the University of Michigan, Ann Arbor, and received his MA and PhD in Political Science. He was a lecturer in political science at the University of Michigan from 1970–71, after which he returned home to Jamaica to be a lecturer at the University of the West Indies. He rose through the ranks of the university to senior lecturer in government (1974–78) to reader in political sociology (1978–83) to be a professor of political sociology (1983–93).

Many of you knew Carl as social scientist, pollster, colleague, newspaper columnist, author, and academic. He was all of those things, but he was also my husband, and I am writing this account as a wife writing about her relationship with her husband.

The perculation for this manuscript has been many years in the making. Effort was necessary, endurance was essential, and energy both physical and mental, was needed to complete this task. All of these ingredients were not always present together in the quantity required, until now.

To family and friends, both mine and his, who love us and would prefer that some of these events remain private, I hope that by the time you have finished reading this extremely personal account, you would have understood.

FIRE DEH A MUS MUS TAIL, 'IM TINK A COOL BREEZE

When you think all is well, trouble looms

THERE ARE TIMES when the universe offers up clues as to what is about to happen in one's life. One might feel a strange pang, a momentary shiver, a deep sigh that seems to originate at the unconscious level, a heavy feeling in the pit of one's stomach, a laden spirit, a misting of the eyes with threatening tears, a foreboding about attending an event. None of these clues were offered to me as my family and I got dressed to attend the Third World Concert on December 29, 1991.

There I was, 44 years old and married since 1975. I had left my full-time teaching job at the Norman Manley Secondary School and was a stay-at-home mom, teaching part-time occasionally. My husband was a university professor, a newspaper columnist at the *Daily Gleaner* and a well-known and highly respected political pollster, having founded the Carl Stone Polls.

Our family's Christmas celebrations had gone well and now the year 1991 was winding down. Every year, my siblings and I, along with our families, gathered at Momma and Daddy for Christmas Dinner. As always, when the extended family gathers, the shared memories and the mix of personalities, intermingled with the pleasure of us all being together with some good food, make for great festivity. Throughout the season, Carl, the children and I, visited many friends delivering and receiving gifts. I was looking forward to the New Year's Eve partying in a couple of days, but tonight Carl and I were at our home in Kingston preparing to attend the Third World concert at the Courtleigh Manor Hotel. Our children, Tricia, age 12 and Timothy, age 8, were coming along but I was having second thoughts about taking them.

'Carl, are you sure it's a good idea to take the children, I mean the crowds and it is outdoors and all that.' I watched him as he stood in front of the dresser in our bedroom buttoning up his shirt. He knitted his brows then turned to me.

'What are you talking about Rose? There is a lot of rubbish parading as music nowadays,' he said. 'I want to expose them to some good Reggae music, and talk with them after the concert to explain the finer points of it. It is not a problem.' He glanced in the mirror and headed towards the bathroom. I followed him.

'But remember the time when we took them to Portland for the jazz festival, the crowd was dense and it...'

'Rained? Yes, it rained,' he said, finishing off for me. 'If it rains this time, it will still be no problem.'

I stood in the doorway and watched as he brushed his teeth.

'Just as long as you know that it is your responsibility to take them to the bathroom and deal with them and the crowd, especially if they want to go home. Remember, Carl, I am going there to enjoy the music,' stressing the word *music.*

He mumbled something and smiled which told me he had accepted my terms.

Stephen 'Cat' Coore, Bunny Rugs, Michael 'Ibo' Cooper and the gang would all be there at the hotel to take us on a musical voyage to Reggae heaven. By 1991 they had already made waves in the international music community, and whenever they played in Jamaica, sold out crowds of Jamaicans would flock to see them. Later, as we travelled the short distance to the venue Carl's enthusiasm further energized the children about going to the concert. He smiled at me. I slapped him playfully on his leg.

I felt elated that Carl was excited about going to the concert. When he was in this mood he was a delight to be around. He was smiling and relaxed. He had lost a few pounds recently and looked content, virile and the picture of health.

As we entered the crowded hotel, the band was just striking up the first few notes of 'Jah Glory'. A friend, Sharon, a teacher like me who also chose to stay at home with her two sons, and her husband, an attorney who I knew, greeted us. Sharon and her family were one of a group of families that we occasionally vacationed with on Jamaica's North Coast. Smiling all the time, we carefully picked our way through the throng of music-loving Jamaicans. No chairs were provided and none were needed because Third World's music was too infectious to sit through. It was pure raw Jamaican reggae and dance music and already I could see Carl snapping his fingers. He hoisted Timothy to his shoulders. Carl was a very fit man at 51 years old. Despite a recent diabetic scare, he was still jogging and playing tennis in the mornings.

The haunting rhythm of the reggae held the crowd and all we could do was rock to the beat and immerse ourselves in its healing. Any stress I had as a mother raising two young children floated away as I swayed along with everyone else. I felt close to Carl even though I was lost in the music. When he lifted Timothy down from his shoulders, something made me move closer to him. Even above the loudness of the music, I heard him say to our son, 'Daddy is a bit tired.' 'How unusual,' I thought. Recently I had participated in the annual Jamaica Carnival. Carl, Tricia and Timothy walked the two mile distance from our home to catch a glimpse of me as my group passed by. All the while there and back home, Timothy was on Carl's shoulders. But at that moment, he did not look himself. I noticed that he was no longer swaying to the music, and I placed my mouth close to his ear.

'Are you OK?' I asked, finding it strange for him to be tired so easily.

'Yes, I will just rest a while then I will lift him again.' My insides were palpitating but I was in a sea of humanity dancing their troubles away and this was not the time to show panic. With my arms around his waist I spoke into his ear again.

'Maybe you shouldn't lift him all the way to your shoulders Carl.'

'It's OK, I am fine.'

I examined his face for signs – signs of what, I couldn't have said. After 16 years of marriage I knew when something was wrong, so I remained close to him. I turned my eyes to the stage, to 'Cat' Coore on the cello, but my soul was no longer with the music. After about ten minutes I saw Timothy again hold up his hands to his father. Carl bent down and picked him up, then swung him onto his shoulders. In almost the same motion, Timothy was back down. Panic was threatening to set in but I was telling myself to remain calm as the music, loud and thumping as it was, disappeared from my world. I instinctively moved closer to Carl.

'Are you OK?' I asked again, searching his face, his eyes. This time it could not be hidden. 'I don't feel so well,' he admitted. 'I feel a little strange.'

I heard strangeness in his voice too. I held him close, and then in much less than a minute I felt his body weight against me. I held on to him, fearing that he might faint. I looked around and I saw a couple seated on chairs that they must have carried from home. After a couple of minutes Carl seemed to be reviving. He stood a little straighter and his body was no longer heavy against mine. I used the opportunity to speak to the woman.

'My husband is not feeling well. Can you allow him to sit for a while?'

Without hesitation she gave up the chair and I got Carl seated. His head was lowered and I feared that he would fall off the chair. I stood behind him with my arms holding him against the back of the chair. I tried to talk to him but he did not respond.

'Carl, Carl, can you hear me?'

After a while Carl started responding to me.

'Yes Rose, I hear you.'

I left the children with him, telling them to watch out for Daddy because he was not feeling well. I rushed off to find Sharon. When I found her I explained that Carl was not well. She was always well equipped for situations like this.

'You people are always telling me what an old lady I am for carrying around these things with me all the time, but here you are.'

She handed me a small container of Wray and Nephew white rum and a handkerchief. I thanked her and went back to Carl. After wetting the handkerchief with the rum I placed it close to his nose. Carl stared up at me in a daze, almost as if he did not recognize me. Then he attempted to stand. He slumped back in the chair. As I grasped his body and wiped his face and neck with the wet kerchief, I realized that he had fainted.

Earlier I had feared the crowd might create problems for my young children. Now that very crowd protected me. I was in the middle, being pressed on, but few were aware of my plight. Trying to act inconspicuous and, even more important, trying my best not to alarm the children, I feigned conversation with Carl. He slowly started to come around. Seeming confused at first, he looked around, then at me, again with that peculiar stare. With my mouth to his ear I asked, 'Are you feeling any better?'

He leaned his head towards me, and asked, 'What happened?'

'You fainted. Must have done too many laps this morning,' I said.

For a few seconds he allowed my words to sink in. 'Oh boy,' he said then shook his head then sighed.

I told him to relax, that I would arrange to get him home. I told the children to remain by their father.

Without my knowing it, an acquaintance of ours had

seen most of what had happened. Ali McNab, a journalist and businessman, came over just as I was moving off to find Sharon. He whispered in my ear, 'Mrs Stone, I'm here if you need me.'

I was surprised but so grateful and my spirit started to lift. 'Thanks,' I said as I continued to head towards Sharon. I found her and told her that I was leaving, though I didn't know how I would make my way through the crowd.

When I returned, I was relieved to see Carl talking with the children. I felt as if a dark cloud had dissipated. I began to smile again, but still had not figured out how to leave the venue. What if he fainted again? I gazed around and saw Ali coming towards us. He was with another acquaintance of Carl's, Ruddy Spencer, a trade unionist and politician.

'Mrs Stone, I believe he overdid it this morning at tennis,' said McNab in a reassuring voice.

'I have to get him home now.'

'Yes, I know. We saw what happened. Let me and Ruddy walk with Carl and you deal with the children.' Carl got up and appeared ok. I thanked the couple for the use of the chair. As Ali and Ruddy started talking to Carl, I took hold of the children's hands and told them that Daddy was feeling better but we had to leave. We glanced back and saw Ali to Carl's right and Ruddy to his left. I was comforted that we might reach the car without incident. Unable to look back at Carl because of the density of the crowd, I held on tight to the children's hands and forged through the throng.

After we returned from the Third World concert, Carl went straight upstairs while I brewed some garlic tea for him. He sat on the bed and drank it, wondering aloud whether his blood pressure had shot up suddenly and caused him to faint. I asked him about the doctor he had seen recently about his blood pressure who told him he might have diabetes.

'Carl, did the doctor give you a time when the test results would be ready?'

'Yes. It should be ready about now.'

'Did he actually tell you that you have diabetes?'

'No. He didn't say that I have diabetes. He said that I might be pre-diabetic and so that's why he told me to cut back on fruits in particular and sweets in general, just in case.'

'Why did he decide to test for diabetes?'

'He decided to do a general check up and had some concerns.'

I made a mental note to call that doctor on Red Hills Road as soon as possible.

I walked downstairs to the back patio, then up the stairs again. I checked on the children who were by then asleep in their beds. My brain was working overtime, just thinking, thinking. I made my way slowly along the passage back to the master bedroom. Carl was now sleeping peacefully. Sitting in the rocking chair, looking at my husband as he slept, I went over in my mind some of the events in our lives that brought us to this place.

BUD CYAAN FLY PON ONE WING

It is wise to strike a balance in all things

AT THE AGE OF 16 I fantasized about my life as a woman. This woman would be the best teacher. After working in Jamaica for a short time she would travel the world working in Australia and New Zealand and have many affairs in Switzerland. My fantasy of this idealized woman would help to shape the real woman I would become over the next three decades. Sometimes fantasy and reality converged, but only for short periods. More often the fantasy mocked me.

I met Carl the summer of 1974 before beginning the final year of my BA General at the University of the West Indies (UWI). I did courses in management studies and sociology which meant that I had practical experience as an interviewer. He was a lecturer in the department of government at the time and was looking for students to work as interviewers for a summer project on Land Lease Development in Jamaica. I applied, was interviewed by him and got the job. That summer Carl and I spent a lot of time together interviewing farmers all over Jamaica.

By the end of summer we had become very good friends. I had found a male friend who I could share everything about my life with, without feeling judged. He reciprocated this sharing and we both marvelled at the symbiosis that occurred when we were together. By the end of my final year Carl and I had fallen in love with each other. I fell in love with Carl because he saw and understood who I really was. Physically, he embodied all that I needed. I had started to rethink the issues of freedom and marriage. We got married in June 1975. I was 27 years old and Carl was 35.

After graduating from UWI, I taught at Norman Manley Junior Secondary School. While there I took the time to complete a postgraduate diploma in education (DipEd). This 'in service' training allowed me to teach full time and be released from classes every Friday for a year for practical training. The theoretical part of the course was done the following summer. I eventually rose to become head of the English department.

During those first five years of our marriage, 1975–80, Jamaica was in political upheaval. Carl was conducting political polls and writing regular columns for the *Daily Gleaner*. The polls showed that the governing People's National Party (PNP) led by Michael Manley was losing support to the Edward Seaga-led Jamaica Labour Party (JLP) opposition. While I saw Carl's columns as being objective, some readers saw them as having an anti-PNP stance. By 1980 political temperatures ran very hot and Carl, whose 'Carl Stone Polls' showed the opposition ahead, was seen as a traitor and enemy by many PNP supporters. After a poll was published, it was not unusual for Carl and me to receive threatening phone calls. The phone calls frightened me, and while I did not feel personally at risk, I feared that his life certainly was.

It was within this context that in October of 1980 I received a phone call from the principal of Norman Manley Secondary School. I had resigned my teaching post at the end of the previous school year to stay at home with my daughter Tricia, who was 16 months old at the time. Because I had many friends at Norman Manley, I had visited the school occasionally in September and October.

'Mrs Stone, I have something serious to say to you. I have had discussions with my two vice principals about a particular matter concerning you.' I listened, not responding in any way. 'In fact, we were wondering whether we should tell you or not. What happened was, just this week a crowd of women showed up at our school gate asking for the wife of Carl Stone. Apparently they did not know that you don't teach here any more.'

I responded for the first time, with a simple, 'Uh huh.'

'They were insisting that we let them in. These women had machetes and ice picks and they were very boisterous. Mrs Stone, for your safety I am asking you not to visit here for a while'.

I thanked him for calling and hung up. Even in retrospect it is still difficult to understand that they would use me to get to Carl. I shudder to think what would have happened if I had driven up that day with Tricia in the car.

As I sat watching Carl sleep after the Third World concert, I pondered political tribalism. I also wondered what Carl's fainting spell was all about and if there was any connection to past illnesses.

In 1977, two years after our marriage Carl had been

head of a tribunal looking into industrial relations concerns at Jamaica Flour Mills. One day he complained of a painful headache, I applied an icepack, gave him painkillers, and then suggested he sleep for a while. That afternoon he was supposed to attend the tribunal. In the evening when he awoke, he was very upset with me for not waking him in time. To Carl, it was the worst thing I could have done. The media carried the story that the head of the Flour Mills tribunal had failed to show up. Carl was not amused.

Later when the headache returned, I forced him to see a doctor. His blood pressure was so high that the doctor recommended immediate hospitalization. He spent four days at the University Hospital where they used medication to carefully and gradually bring his blood pressure down. Over the years Carl had astounded medical personnel by his shunning of medication and his successful use of diet and exercise to bring his blood pressure down to normal. One doctor, however, had concerns. She pointed out that there could be times when, even though his levels might return to normal, the absence of medication would prevent his system from being able to deal with these spikes in blood pressure.

The high blood pressure incident just two years after we got married was the only major medical problem Carl had had. He seemed to battle it successfully with diet and exercise, so I was astounded when, in October 1991, a doctor told him he might be diabetic. He was advised to cut back on fruit, something he loved. When he subsequently lost some weight, I thought nothing of it because he had reduced his sugar intake. It came to me that night in 1991 that Dr Errol, an expert on diabetes, had young daughters who were studying ballet at the same school as Tricia. As I sat looking at Carl I thought about using that connection to book an appointment with him.

My thoughts switched from concern about Carl's health to the evening I should have had. Third World was one of my favourite Jamaican vocal bands and I probably would not get to see them again for years. Before we left for the concert I had told Carl that I was going there to enjoy the music, really enjoy it, yet between our arrival at the concert and the time we left would have been no more than 40 minutes. Did I hear my favourite Third World song, 'Reggae Ambassador?' Did 'Cat' Coore do his thing on the cello? In fact, it hit home that I could remember only the first few lines of the first song, 'Jah Glory'. I had set out to enjoy the music, the dancing, the good time and all of the good vibes, but now, all of these seemed so unimportant. They had been eclipsed by my worries about Carl's fainting spell.

I started wondering how Carl would deal with ill heath, given some of the personality traits he had developed through the years. Carl was an incurable workaholic, teaching full time, marking papers, meeting deadlines for the numerous market research surveys he did, and the political polls he conducted for the *Gleaner*, writing two newspaper columns a week and, occasionally, giving speeches at various gatherings. On top of all this, he had to be a father to his growing children, especially Timothy who idolized him. He had to be my husband and, he had to find the time to allow me to be his wife. He also had his morning run and tennis game, and he loved going to nightclubs and bars in Kingston and St. Andrew.

It had become our custom that each anniversary we would leave the children with Momma and my sister Andrea and steal away, the two of us, to the North Coast and spend a weekend in a hotel. In June 1990 we arrived at Sandals, Ocho Rios. As was his terrible habit he carried work with him, and did it right up until the time we reached the hotel. Because he was so tired, when we arrived at 5:00 p.m., Carl had to take a nap. I changed into swimwear and headed for the beach. When I returned to the room sometime later, he was still asleep.

At 10:00 p.m. Carl was still sleeping, and I was upset and disappointed over the difference between how I imagined this weekend to be and how it actually was. We had planned to reach the hotel by a least 2:00 p.m.; we were going to swim for a while and then dress up for dinner. By 10:00 p.m. however, I did not feel like dressing up any longer. When Carl finally woke up at 10:30 p.m. he apologized, and I had to make the decision to be pleasant and not bring up all my issues connected with his 'workaholism'. It was difficult for me to be upset with Carl for sleeping when I knew he was tired, but I certainly had many complaints about how he had set up his life so that there was hardly any time for him to rest.

The next morning, we had breakfast and then strolled down to the beach. The water was calm and the white sand inviting. We saw two empty hammocks and I suggested we lie in them for a while. We were so relaxed, I thought, just lying there, chit chatting, when Carl suddenly said, 'Rose, you are probably the only person in the world I can say this to and I know you won't feel offended by it. This really has nothing to do with you but I have to tell you.'

I turned towards him and looked at him as he continued. 'You see me lying here in this hammock. Rose, I really believe this is a giant waste of time. When I think of all the things I could be doing this just feels like wasting time.'

I had half expected him to say that, and laughed inside. 'Well, you *are* going to waste time for the next two days, and you *are* going to enjoy wasting time, today and tomorrow.'

He reached over to me, an apologetic expression on his face. He held on to my hand and gently squeezed it. Locking his eyes on mine he said, 'I know, Rose, I know.'

Not only did Carl's incurable workaholic tendencies affect our private times together but it also influenced our approach to normal, everyday decisions. Carl knew that I was becoming increasingly dissatisfied with how my life had turned out to be inside the marriage. I had to be fighting too hard for things that were important to me. The fact that I voiced this feeling of discontent should have made Carl sensitive to and give priority to these issues. An example of this had to do with Professor Archie Singham. Archie Singham, as I understood it, was from Cylon (now Sri Lanka) and lectured at the Mona campus of UWI when Carl, and others like him, were there (1964–68). He became a mentor to many of these young men, including Carl.

Many years later, I, along with the children, met Archie on a couple of occasions when he visited Jamaica and sought Carl out. I liked Archie and I thought we all had a good time when we saw each other. He was particularly good with the children. I thought that I saw another facet of Carl when he interacted with Archie; he was comfortable and welcoming with him, relaxed, unhurried, friendly and open – a side of him that I liked a lot. When we heard that Archie was ill and might be dying I immediately thought that Carl and I should go to New York to see him. Carl said he did not have the time, he had a paper to complete. The notion of not having time for a sick friend was like heresy to me. Finally, Carl promised me that he would make time but he never did and I stopped forcing the issue. Archie died of course and I told Carl that under the circumstances I would not be attending the funeral; neither did he.

My last thoughts as I lay beside my sleeping husband and put my arms around him were that Carl's personality and lifestyle were at odds with being ill. While we still had an active and loving marriage, in spite of all our issues, I wondered how a possibly new challenge would impact us and how we would find the 'oomph' to muddle through.

COW DEH A PASTURE 'IM NUH KNOW SEH BUTCHER A WATCH 'IM

Who is to know when there is danger lurking?

I DECIDED THAT I WAS GOING to start my investigations into the cause of Carl's collapse at the concert so I called the doctor on Red Hills Road who had told him that he might be diabetic, thinking I would bring him up to date. As I had expected, I was totally stonewalled: the doctor would not speak to me. At times like this, as had happened in the past, I got so outraged by the double standard for women. I believed that if the tables were reversed and Carl was calling, and I was the one who was ill, a doctor would be more forthcoming.

I did the next best thing; I got the doctor on the phone and asked Carl to speak to him to get the results of the tests that had been done. The doctor told him that he was not diabetic that he just needed some iron. Cutting out sugars, especially fruit, had been a complete waste of time and Carl had lost all that weight for nothing. I still believed that we needed to get to Dr Errol.

I was able to make an appointment for January 4, 1992. I spoke to Carl beforehand, told him that I was going to be aggressive in my attempt to find out what was wrong with him, and got an assurance from him that he would not object to this. Leading up to the appointment, I experienced a roller coaster of emotions in trying to read what Carl's body was trying to tell him about his health. Carl resumed his normal activities the day after he had fainted, working in his office for hours. The only promise I got him to make was that he would not do any physical activity such as jogging, playing tennis or working out. He reluctantly complied.

By now our friends knew about Carl's incident at the concert and had started to show their concern by calling and visiting us. We were closest to Lisa and Phillip. I first met Lisa through my sister, Shirley when we were teenagers. Even though I was four years older than her, we were a part of a group of friends who lived in the same area in Kingston. We went to parties together, had group dates, and generally had a wonderful time as our friendships developed and deepened. As a group, we all supported Lisa when she entered and won the Miss Jamaica (World) competition in the 1970s and went to represent Jamaica at the Miss World competition in London. We remained friends through each others' engagements, marriages and entry into motherhood. Lisa and I became very close and when she got married to Phillip, the friendship extended to include our husbands. Lisa, like me, had left her job as a banker to stay home with her three children. Her husband, Phillip, is an attorney-at-law. As two couples, we had celebrated New Years Eve together for the past 18 years. The four of us discussed our annual New Year's Eve celebration and wondered if it was a good idea for Carl to attend. Carl assured us that he was feeling better and that he would be at the party.

We attended the party at the Matalons, a successful Jamaican business family who hosted a New Year's Eve party annually at one of their residences in Jack's Hill; an upscale community in St. Andrew, Jamaica. At that point Carl had not been indulging in liquor for several months because of his diabetic scare, but at the party he had quite a few drinks. He surprised our group of friends and me by dancing all night, and at 4:00 a.m. he still wanted to dance with me. I found this truly amazing when I considered what had happened three days ago at the Third World concert.

The whirl of emotions continued. Carl's brother Leroy and his family vacationed in Jamaica every year around this time. They live in Ottawa, Canada, and also own a house, 'Rivera', in Mammee Bay along the north coast of Jamaica. We were expected to visit 'Rivera' and spend some time with the family. Carl and I talked about going on January 2nd, but Carl said he didn't feel he could make it, he felt tired. I wondered if tiredness was the real reason or he just wanted to delay the inevitable visit with his family. Even though he looked forward to this time with his family, he was always reluctant to disrupt his work schedule.

As it turned out, Carl really was not feeling well. I had to drive to Mammee Bay on January 3rd. Carl looked ill. The loss of weight that seemed so attractive to me on New Year's Eve on the dance floor now looked ominous. Carl's mother, Flossie, was distressed when she saw her son, as were Leroy and his wife Susan. I told them about the doctor's appointment the next day and reassured them that we were going to try our best to get to the bottom of Carl's problem. Carl spent the day lying on a large lounge chair, frequently dozing off, sometimes conversing with Leroy or trying to answer his mother's many questions about his health.

I drove Carl and the children back to Kingston that evening from Mammee Bay with a sense that tomorrow, and the doctor's appointment, could not come quickly enough. Carl was quiet and withdrawn, smiling only in order not to frighten the children. He explained to them that he was going to the doctor the next day and that the doctor would help him to feel better.

By the time we reached Dr Errol, Carl was in bad shape. We went into the doctor's office together as pre-arranged. The doctor asked questions and Carl answered, but I decided that the answers were not full enough, nor were they giving us all the pertinent information.

At one point I tried to say something, but Carl interjected, 'Remember Rose, I am the one who is ill.' I took a deep breath, wondering if Carl and I were going to have a quarrel right there in front of the doctor. This certainly was a possibility, because I was going to make sure that the doctor had all the details and specifically all the information on what brought us to his office. Dr Errol read the situation well, however, and his handling of it prevented a quarrel. He listened intently while Carl gave him answers. When he was finished with Carl, he turned to me. 'Mrs Stone, do you have anything to add to this?' I was so grateful to find a sensible doctor, and so I told him what I thought, most of which Carl had thought was insignificant and left out. He told the doctor that he had tonsillitis and that he had fainted at the Third World concert. He did not mention the frequency of his bouts with tonsillitis or how often he had slipped in and out of consciousness at the concert.

After Dr Errol had examined Carl, he told us he did not like a lot of the indicators but that he had to do more tests before he could give us a definitive diagnosis. He also told us that he was almost sure Carl did not have diabetes, that something else had caused Carl to look and feel as he did. Carl had to undergo several blood tests and we were to come back for the results. He was given a prescription, which included medication for high blood pressure – something he had not taken for over ten years – and antibiotics because he had a fever. The doctor advised him that he was to rest as much as possible and predicted that he would begin to feel better in a couple of days.

As I left the doctor's office that day I was beginning to see what my friend Lisa had noticed and commented on a couple of months earlier when she thought Carl's weight loss looked more serious than what one would expect in a person coming off sugar. And to add to my worry, the doctor's reaction had given me the subtle impression that Carl's symptoms indicated he was very ill, and might have been sick for a long time.

I had lovingly suggested to Carl that he not work so hard, had even beseeched him. His work ethic had grown so all consuming over the years that sometimes when we had social activities he was so tired that we did not attend. Many times he was so frazzled by his attempt to do as much work as possible before an event that he ended up not feeling well. I wondered if his ill health was connected to his having tonsillitis every couple of months, usually accompanied by a fever. On reflection it seemed to me that when Carl tried to relax or rest after working non-stop for days, he would fall ill with tonsillitis. Carl would go to various doctors, get antibiotics, and then would seem back to normal in a couple of days. I had spoken about this tonsillitis problem with his mother, and Flossie had calmed any fears I had by telling me Carl had had this problem since he was a child. A doctor had advised her that it unnecessary to have the tonsils removed.

Friends and family called or visited to comfort and give advice. My friend Carmen came to visit Carl. I met Carmen in 1987 when she owned and operated a boutique in Kingston. She had some ideas as to what Carl could do to lower his blood pressure. She also brought a juice extractor and encouraged us to use it with vegetables.

W'EN YUH YEYE DEEP YUH CRY IN TIME
When you foresee tragedy, start facing it early

'ROSE,' SAID CARL ON OUR DRIVE to Dr Errol a few days later, 'as we are getting closer to the doctor's office I am starting to get more and more worried. I just can't imagine what he is going to say to us.'

'The only way to explain how I feel is that my whole body is a heart beat and it is pulsating so rapidly that I can hardly breathe or walk,' I replied.

'We have to try to quiet our thoughts and believe that anything Dr Errol tells us, we can get through.'

'You know, Carl, how I have to think about this, is that hundreds of people have gone through, and are going through, this kind of challenge – and if they could do it so can we.'

When we arrived, we parked and walked into the waiting area. In a few minutes Carl's name was called and we entered Dr Errol's office. As we shook hands and greeted each other, the doctor spoke directly to Carl.

'Professor, the test results are alarming but let me ask this. How long do you think you have been unwell?'

'To be truthful, not very long,' said Carl. 'I think I started to feel a little tired when I came off my fruits and cut out sugars. But I was able to do all my exercises every morning. When I felt tired, I rested and felt completely normal afterwards.'

'Have you given any further thoughts to lessening your work load, if even for a while?'

'I have been thinking about that very seriously but I will attend to that as the need arises.'

'What about your drinking – do you have that under control? The last time we met, you mentioned that you had stopped drinking for a while. Most of the medication that you will have to take prohibits drinking.'

'I can stop drinking now if I have to. The only person that thinks my drinking is out of control is Rose, but even she has to admit that I stopped drinking for over three months when I got the diabetes scare.'

I had been unable to find my voice until now.

'Carl, if you stop drinking altogether, how will you get your information to write?'

'Doc, Rose is very sceptical when I tell her that I feel comfortable and at ease in bars not only because of the camaraderie and liquor, but because I get my best material for my columns right there in the "belly of the beast". But I would change that immediately if my health is at risk.'

'Carl, how are you feeling today? Did the medication help in any way?'

'Yes Doc, my throat is feeling better, so I suspect the temperature is gone. My achy and woozy head, I don't have any more. The dizziness I still get from time to time. Probably the blood pressure is a little more under control. I still feel unusually tired, but I believe that as soon as I can exercise again, that will help.'

'I am so sorry to have to tell you this but my findings from the test results suggest that you might have myeloma, which as you know is cancer of the bone marrow. This is not conclusive – further tests need to be done. I am going to send your notes off to Dr Grace who works out of Medical Associates. She is an excellent doctor for diseases such as these and I believe she will be a good fit for you. I am expecting a call from a colleague who I asked to consult with me on this matter just to see if my diagnosis is on the right track.' Just then, the phone rang. 'This might be him now, so excuse me.'

My body is rigid. I can't believe that Carl is going to die soon. His aunt died in 1985 of myeloma too. I witnessed and participated in the journey of her illness from the beginning until the end. I was there with Carl's mother, Flossie, at University Hospital when her sister died. Could it be that she will have to go through the same thing with her son? Will my children lose their father? It is not possible that I have to go through this again and worse of all, lose my husband.

As the doctor accepts the phone call and repeats some numbers from Carl's test results to the person at the other end, I look at Carl, but I cannot read anything from his face. Dr Errol ends his phone call. 'Dr. Errol, when will the other doctor receive Carl's file?' I asked. 'I will send it down right away, so she will get it by tomorrow morning.' The Doctor is reassuring. As we leave his office, he tells us that we can call him anytime. Still, I am stunned by what we have just been told. I try to control my breathing and my emotions. I try to do this for Carl's sake, but right now he looks more accepting and in control that I am.

As we walk out into the lobby, Carl takes both my hands in his, looks into my eyes and says, 'Don't worry Rose, we are going to fight this. You are not getting rid of me this easily.'

And he smiles. I am grateful for his optimism and wish that I could find even a small thread of it in myself.

That evening I was restless. I needed more information. I wanted to talk to Dr Errol privately. My friend, Lisa, and my youngest sister, Andrea, were with me at home debating the issue. What I really wanted to do was ask Dr Errol how long Carl had to live. Lisa was of the opinion that this was not a good idea, that the truth could only hurt me. Andrea believed that if I wanted to do this very badly, then I should.

'Lisa, let me try to explain to you how I feel. Right now on this 16th day of January 1992, I feel that Carl is going to die soon. I need to prepare every cell in my body for this eventuality. If I don't, I can't cope. I need to know.'

'You seem to think that the doctors are gods, but I don't,' she said. 'They don't know everything and they might give you false information.'

'Lisa, I am an intelligent woman. Right now I am overwrought but I am still thinking coherently. I know how to ask the question, and certainly the doctor knows

how to answer me. I don't need a specific time and date but I need to know his estimation as a professional.'
'You are making the wrong decision. I think if it is going to happen it will happen whether you talk to the doctor or not'.

Andrea interjected, 'Rose, if you really feel strongly that you need this information you should get it.'

'Why can't you wait and deal with it when it comes?' Lisa continued.

'Lisa Marie, I, Rosemarie Wignall Stone, need to know this. I need knowledge to help me to cope, so I am going to the doctor's office now. Please take me there or I will make other arrangements.'

She drove Andrea and me to the doctor's office. I had called before to verify whether he was in office. As I did not have an appointment, I had to wait a few minutes before I could see him. I asked him what I needed to know. In return he asked me some questions. He really talked to me. I was grateful for his understanding of my need. He gave me the information for which I had come. What I didn't know was whether my body could withstand the pain of his revelations.

As I left the office, Lisa and Andrea tried to talk to me and I mouthed some words but the sounds would not come out. I started to walk hurriedly away from them. I needed to get to the car. I ran to the car park and as I neared the vehicle, my feet weakened. I fell to my knees, folded my arms around my body and lowered my head. I cried and cried and cried. I could feel waves of pain wash over me. Andrea and Lisa tried to console me but I was oblivious to them.

Someone else was coming into the parking area, so I quickly straightened my back and got up. I tried to walk and look normal. The tears, however, were beyond my control. I realized that I must pull myself together, and I only had a short time to do so; the doctor's office was two minutes drive from home. I had to go home to Carl and the children and pretend that this meeting had not taken place. On the short journey home Andrea tried to comfort me.

'Rose, you will get through this. We are all here for you.'

Lisa was angry with me and began to voice this.

'I cannot understand anybody who goes out of their way to hurt themselves. I just cannot understand you. Look at the state you are in now.'

'This is the way I choose to handle it. I know myself and my coping mechanisms. Lisa I have to trust my instincts. I don't know any other way.'

'We are just beginning to find out about Carl's illness and I must tell you that I think you have the wrong approach to this. If you continue like this you will get sick too and maybe even die before him.'

At home as we are getting out of the car, I thought to myself that after all these years of friendship with Lisa, she just did not understand me. I am grateful that my sister was here. Even if she did not agree with my way of doing things, she defended my right to do them.

As I turned my thoughts to the future, I thought about turns in the road of life.

My husband Carl was very ill and might die soon.
He was about to face the hardest struggle of his life.
My two young children were about to lose their father.
How in the world was I going to make it through this?

A NUH DI SAME DAY LEAF DRAP INNA WATA I' ROTTEN

A misdeed can have dire consequences many years later

THE SPOTLIGHT FOR THE PAST TWO WEEKS had been placed directly on Carl's ill health and our attempts to investigate and try to bring him back physically to a place where he might recover. The doctors were an integral part of this search. In our continued quest I called Dr Grace, as Dr Errol had suggested. Dr Grace and I spoke for a while and I tried to give her some background on Carl's illness. She told me she had received the files and that Carl had an appointment for the afternoon of January 20th.

Meanwhile, our family also had to deal with the everyday matters of going to work and school. I was teaching part time at New Vision Prep School. At this time I was working from 8:00 a.m. to 12:00 p.m. helping the Common Entrance class which had exams towards the end of January, at which time I planned stop teaching. It was very important for me to be at home with the children. Teaching provided a respite from the challenges we were facing and I was fulfilling a responsibility to the children, myself and to my friend Carol N. who had founded the school. My son Timothy also attended New Vision Prep. Tricia had to return to school at St. Hugh's High.

In the afternoons, apart from answering calls and

receiving visits from friends I faced the immediate and real problem of dealing with Carl's mother. Mother (the name we all called Flossie) had become increasingly anxious about her son's health. She was still in Mammee Bay with her son Leroy and his family. I had kept Leroy up to date on all the medical news and had left the decision of telling Mother about the diagnosis to Carl and Leroy. Mother and I had always enjoyed such a close relationship that many of my friends marvelled at, but as soon as Carl became ill I realized that the relationship would have to change. It was too much for me. In the past, it had not been unusual for Mother and me to have at least three short conversations daily. But the substance of our conversations changed entirely after Carl was diagnosed: she became fixated on his health. Her calls were especially draining for me because they were accompanied by moans, groans and tears.

Early in January, when I realized that it was not going to work for me emotionally and psychologically to have these conversations, I had a frank discussion with her. I explained to her about how exhausting it was for me to keep talking about Carl's illness. I tried to keep the effects of these calls to myself, but Carl noticed and told me to tell Mother that she should speak directly to him or Leroy. I knew that Mother had just as many close friends as I did, so I suggested that she choose a couple of friends to talk to when she had the need. When she wanted information she could always talk to Carl and Leroy.

Mother continued her calls to me.

One morning there was a knock on my classroom

door. I looked up and the secretary said, 'There is a call for you Mrs Stone.' I was startled. I wanted to run to the telephone but my legs would not allow it. My insides were quivering. I hoped my emotions were not visible to the children and teachers as I passed them on the way to take the call in the main office. I looked up at the clock; it was 8:40 a.m. This had to be an emergency; no one would normally call me at this time in the morning while I was teaching. My first thoughts were of Carl and then Tricia. I picked up the telephone. 'Hello.' I tried to stay calm.

'Hi Rose, I hope I am not disturbing you.'

'Hi Mother, how are you?' I hoped nothing had happened to her either.

'Rose. I was just wondering,' she moaned and I knew what this call was about.

'Mother, I can't do this now, this is not the time. I am at school, I am teaching. We have spoken about this many times before.'

'Rose, I won't take much time. I want to know if you are giving Carl his vitamins.' I took a deep breath knowing she would hear my annoyance but hoping this would signal to her to end her questioning.

'Mother…,' I was trying to breathe evenly.

'Rose, I just want to know if you are giving Carl his fruits and vegetables. He needs his fruits and vegetables.'

I paused for control. Both of us knew that Carl was over 50 years old. I did not say all that I was thinking. I knew she was under a lot of stress.

'Mother…,' my breathing was shallow now.

'What about his diet Rose?' she continued. I heard the

tears in her voice. Mother knew about Carl's diet. For over ten years now I had spoken to her at least three times a day. Unwelcome thoughts that seem to contradict these hours of conversation intrude. As tears started to trickle down my face, the secretary looked up at me, then averted her attention, swivelled her chair away and walked discreetly from the office.

'Mother, this is too much for me and for you. This is not good for either of us. Have you spoken to Carl this morning?'

'Yes, I just did. But Rose I have to know,' she pleaded.

'We have spoken about this already Mother, we can't do this together.' All my misgivings about this situation were being realized as I struggled for control and oxygen.

'Mother, I have to go now, my class is waiting.' I felt the anger beginning to take hold of me but I could not be angry with my mother-in-law. I loved her and we had been friends. She could not or just did not want to do it my way.

'Rose, have you checked his blood pressure? You just have to look after him,' she persisted.

'Mother, I know you well and I thought you knew me too. I want you to listen very carefully to what I have to say.'

'Rose....,' she was crying now.

'Mother, I love your son, I loved your son when he wanted to be loved, when he needed to be loved and also when he didn't deserve to be loved. I know that you know about the vitamins, the diet, the checking of the blood pressure and everything. You know that I do all of those things. What I don't understand is being asked about them at 9 o'clock on a Monday morning while I am in the classroom. You could easily have asked Carl. Mother, you have to trust me that I will do what has to be done.'

'OK Rose, I am sorry to have taken up your time.'

Exhausted, I tried my legs to see if I had the strength to return to the classroom. As I got up I glanced at the clock: 8:43 a.m. I could not believe that only three minutes had passed. I should have been grateful that the call from Mother had taken only a short time. I felt so worn out, so depleted of energy and enthusiasm that if the call had lasted one minute more I felt that I would not have been able to return to the classroom.

Monday, January 20, 1992

Carl and I met with Dr Grace. She went through Carl's results with us. She, like Dr Errol, was amazed that Carl was not more symptomatic than he was. She believed that Dr Errol's diagnosis was correct but said she needed to do some more tests. First would be the bone-marrow biopsy to confirm myeloma. We both liked Dr Grace, we liked her 'bedside manner', her gentleness and everything about her. Carl in particular was in sync with her because they both shared a love of politics and they even managed to slip a little political humour into that rather serious afternoon.

Carl and I visited Dr Grace's office at the Blood Bank and she performed the bone-marrow biopsy. She told me to call her for the results. We then visited Dr Freddy for an ultra sound on Carl's vital organs. I spoke to Dr Freddy in private and got the impression that Carl's heart and his kidney were not in good shape. And so my despair continued.

I walked out of Dr Freddy's office with tears brimming in my eyes. As I drove out of the parking area unto Ripon Road, the tears started to fall in earnest. Carl asked me to stop the car so that we could talk.

'Rose, why are you so upset, what did Dr Freddy say?'

'Your heart … your kidneys … he says they are not in good shape.' I could barely speak as I struggled to catch my breath.

'You are getting too upset Rose, are you sure you can drive?'

'Just give me a minute. I will, shortly. I need some water … something to drink.'

'I promise you that I am going to fight this disease with all that I have. Dr Freddy told me he will help me too. Please don't cry. Remember I have told you that you are not going to get rid of me so easily.'

My worst fear erupted, 'You cannot leave me now Carl, I cannot manage without you! You have to be here to help me with the children!' I gripped him with an urgency born out of my desperation.

'I want to be here for the children too. So let us fight this thing together. And promise me you will wait until I am really leaving to cry like this again.'

'I can't promise you that.' I took a deep breath, 'I think I am OK to drive now.'

As I continued along Ripon Road en route to Lady Musgrave Avenue where Carl wanted to stop to cancel an appointment he had, I knew in my heart that Carl was going to die soon. All the indicators and tests, what I saw when I looked at him, what I was hearing from the doctors, all shared the undercurrent of very bad news for Carl. I hoped I was mistaken and that something would happen to make the feeling of doom go away. As I parked the car on Lady Musgrave Avenue and Carl got out, I watched him walk away from me. I tried to turn my thoughts around and see optimism and hope, but these thoughts were short lived and futile. I closed all the windows and wept. When Carl returned, the windows were foggy, I was overcome. My face felt swollen, my throat ached, my stomach had become a cavern – hollow and echoing, and my limbs felt strange – borrowed, but not the right fit. Carl opened the car door and held out his arms saying, 'Rose you have to stop crying like this, we are going to get through this, hundreds of people all over the world face similar situations.' He hugged me and I hugged him back with all the strength I could muster. The hug did nothing to ease my pessimistic thoughts. We got out of the car and Carl held my hand as we walked a few yards to where a coconut vendor was stationed.

'Two sir? Yu want dem cold?'

'One cold, and three others to take home' Carl said. I looked at him quizzically. 'We will share yours, you usually can't drink one by yourself. I will take mine home and two for the children.'

I drank the coconut water slowly as my throat ached. We walked back to the car and then drove to collect the three coconuts. The vendor gave me the coconut that Carl and I shared, as he had cut it open for me to eat the jelly. I was trying to enjoy the jelly, but halfway through the tears started again. 'Rose…'

'Don't say anything, I am doing better, I am both eating and crying.' I tried to smile through my tears.

Wednesday, January 22, 1992

I called Dr Grace and she told me it was not myeloma. But she wanted Carl to visit Dr Charles, an ear, nose and throat specialist. Through friends of mine I was able to make contact with Dr Charles that very evening at his home and secure an appointment for early the next morning.

Thursday, January 23, 1992

Dr Charles greeted us, looked down on his files and said to my husband, 'Carl, on your last visit you were supposed to do some blood tests, but I do not have the results here, so you remember anything about that?'

'I am not absolutely sure, but I feel I must have done those tests.'

'Dr Charles, I think I remember Carl telling me he did these tests.'

Dr Charles spoke to his nurse, and the search began for the missing test results. In the meantime Dr Charles examined Carl. He looked at his mouth, his ears, his nose and his eyes.

'Carl, how are you feeling now?'

'Much better than how I felt two weeks ago Doc, but I am a bit anxious about the diagnosis. It seems we are having some difficulty in getting to the root of my problem.'

'Carl, can you remember the last period of time that you felt very well?'

'I don't know how to answer that Doc, because I run at least three miles every morning, I play tennis every week and I exercise at least three times a week. I have had no difficulty in my lectures, either preparing them or delivering them and I have been doing a lot of my own personal research lately on a book that I should have begun by now. It is usually on my down time that I get the tonsillitis and the fever. That's what prompted Rose to force me to come to you the last time.'

Dr Charles had been looking intently at Carl as he answered the questions. Then he asked, 'In the last year, that is 1991, can you remember how many times your tonsils got inflamed and you got a fever?'

Carl glanced at me for help but I did not respond because I had an unsettling feeling. I felt uncomfortable and I really believed that Carl should try to answer. He responded, 'Usually when the weather changes a little bit, so probably about three times last year.'

Dr Charles got up from his seat, moved behind Carl and examined his whole neck region again, all the time looking at Carl from different angles. The nurse knocked on the door and told Dr Charles that there are no test results. Dr Charles went back to his desk and flipped through his notes on Carl thoughtfully, then he looked up.

'Carl, actually those test results are not that necessary now, because Dr Grace must have done some new blood tests. But what I want you to do now, is an AIDS test so that we can rule out HIV as a possibility, and then we can go on from there. Do you know Dr Barry up at the University Hospital? I am going to call him now and arrange for you to see him, and he will do the tests. They have a good system at the university that you can go privately and do the test anonymously. You do not have to worry; Dr Barry will look after you well.'

I knew now why I had been feeling as if something life changing was about to take place. The moment Dr Charles said the word *AIDS*, a chill ran through my body and I realized that he had been considering that diagnosis all the time that we were in that office.

Immediately my mind recalled a conversation with Carl, Lisa and myself in which she posed the question to Carl, 'Carl, Rose is always accusing you of infidelity. Can you imagine if you slept with all the women that she has these feelings about? Boy!'
He replied, 'Rose is allowing her imagination to get the better of her. She is being paranoid. I have so much work to do, where would I find time for all of these women?'

As images of that conversation flashed through my mind, I wished for the closeness that Lisa and I once shared because she would understand that my 'imagination' and 'paranoia' have now become my reality.

As we left the office and headed to the car, Carl held on to my hand. Both of us were silent and trembling as we crossed over Tangerine Place.

A few minutes later, in the car, I turned the ignition on and then off. I looked at Carl and asked, 'Is there any likelihood that this test could be positive?'

'Rose let's not make mountains out of molehills right now, let's wait until the test is done. Didn't you hear him say it's just to rule it out?'

'Carl you are an intelligent man, I am an intelligent woman. We have been married for 17 years and so I am asking the question again. Is there any way that this test can be positive?'

'I don't know anybody with AIDS. I have done all sorts of tests and they were OK.'

'Carl, all sorts of tests? Did you do an AIDS test?'

'No. I really don't think we should be upset by this.'

'Did you see how Dr Charles was looking at you?'

'What do you mean?'

'He looked very carefully at you Carl, and I believe he made a clinical diagnosis just now.'

We were quiet for a moment as Carl digested what I had said.

'I am going to ask you for the third time, is there the remotest possibility that this test can be positive?'

'I don't know Rose, I don't know.'

'OK, I will translate that. It means that the test might be positive. We have to proceed on this assumption, and that means that we are not going to tell anyone about the visit to Dr Barry that we are about to embark on. If anyone asks about our day today, it ended after we left Dr Charles' office. Are we agreed?'

'I suppose so.'

I knew that Carl thought it was too early to discuss these practicalities, but I felt the need in every cell of my body, to ensure that we covered up the situation – that we protected ourselves. Submerged below these practicalities were all sorts of feelings that I could not allow to come to the surface at this time. If I so much as loosened, a little, the hold I had on myself, a sea of emotions would overtake me. I stared straight ahead, not daring to blink.

Our drive to Dr Barry's office at the University Hospital was done in silence, both of us immersed in our own thoughts. After we parked and got out of the car, Carl automatically held on to my hand. I was trying hard to present an appearance of normalcy and not let the people we passed on our way in get even a glimpse of what I was feeling inside.

Carl did his best too, that day, laughing and joking through the appointment with Dr Barry.

After we got home, I called my friend Norma, Tricia's ballet teacher, and told her about the 'real' day that we had had. Norma, trained at the Royal Academy, had been teaching ballet for the past 25 years in various schools in Jamaica. She formed The Ballet Centre in 1998 to teach ballet at the semi-professional level. Students with special ability and talent were chosen for these special classes. It was through these special classes that I met John. He was married, a manager of a security company, whose daughters danced with Norma. John and I were on a committee responsible for benefit performances for The Ballet Centre's annual shows. I would organize the participants; residents from children's homes and places of safety, and John would get the private sector sponsorship for these events. I met Shelly in 1982 when Tricia, then three years old, and Jessica aged two (Shelly's first child), were learning to swim with the same instructor. Later at The Ballet Centre, we became friends, after many hours of chauffeuring our children from home to school and to their after-school activities. A huge chunk of our time was spent at The Ballet Centre especially when it was performance time for the students. Shelly was usually in charge of designing and making costumes. These three friends became closer to me as the crisis with Carl's health escalated.

Later that evening as I was in the bedroom, the telephone rang and I answered. The female caller asked to speak to Professor Stone. The voice was familiar but unrecognizable. Carl took the call downstairs and, a few minutes later, came upstairs to me looking troubled. He told me the caller had been Dr Grace, and she had asked him to come to her office by himself in the morning.

'Why would she say this Rose? Isn't that a little unusual? We have been everywhere together and I think she knows that I don't want to hide anything from you. Why would she do this Rose?'

'I don't know Carl.' He sat on the bed, touched my shoulder and said, 'Do you think it's that thing?'

'What thing?'

'That thing, you know what I mean.' He got up and started to pace the room mumbling to himself, 'I can't believe this, I can't believe this. This could not be happening.' He addressed me again, 'What am I to do

Rose?'

'You certainly have to do something because you can't remain in a state like this all night. You are like a caged bird; this is not good for you. Come and sit beside me, come and sit beside me.'

'Rose, I can't wait until tomorrow.'

'You could probably look her up in the directory. She should have a home number. So call her and talk to her.'

He reached for the directory, flipped through some pages and called Dr Grace's home number. We were sitting side by side on the bed as he talked to her. I had my arm around his waist when he said, 'I am a bit worried. Why do you want to see me alone tomorrow?' There was so much anguish in his voice.

He then said, 'I know you are not supposed to give out that kind of information but I can't wait until tomorrow. I have to know tonight. Please Dr Grace, you have to tell me. Is it that thing? Is it AIDS?'

Then Carl let out the loudest scream I have ever heard. 'Oh my God, oh my God, you mean I am not going to live to see my children grow up. Oh Tricia, oh Timothy, what have I done, what have I done?'

Tears streamed down my face as I grabbed Carl around his neck to restrain him and keep him on the bed beside me. While taking the phone from him to talk to Dr Grace, I heard her say 'I am so sorry Professor, I am very, very sorry.' Carl was sobbing in my arms as I listened to her explain how she had arrived at this diagnosis. I told her that we were going to receive at least 20 calls from abroad and numerous local calls because I had told everybody that we would get a diagnosis that day. I also told her that we were not ready to tell the world that Carl had AIDS, so she had to help me by coming up with a plausible alternate diagnosis. She did: cancer of the lymphatic system. She further told me that she had to refer Carl to another doctor whose area of expertise was AIDS. I begged her not to. I pleaded with her to treat Carl and use the doctor as a consultant. After much crying and pleading from me she agreed to keep Carl on as a patient.

That night turned out to be the darkest of my life.

The 'cover up mode' began in earnest as we deceived friends and family about the diagnosis. Fraudulent and cowardly are two words that echoed in my mind. But I knew that I had to be those things that night. I called my sister Andrea and my friend Norma and told them that Carl had cancer of the lymphatic system. I asked Andrea to inform the rest of the family and Norma to call our friends.

We began receiving calls that very night. Carl pulled himself together enough to speak on the telephone to friends and colleagues. I used the time while he was on the phone to remove and hide anything I knew could be used to commit suicide. Carl had gone into such a state that I was frightened for him. He grew worse when the next day, Friday, we visited Dr Grace together.

Dr Grace explained to us the rigours of the disease and again expressed surprise that Carl had worked through so many of the symptoms and much of the discomfort that he must have felt. Carl's blood count, his T-cells and the level of haemoglobin in the blood all suggested that he had contracted HIV at least five years ago. The doctor asked us both some very personal questions about our daily lives together, including our sex lives.

She then turned to me and expressed regret that she had to take some blood from me to test for HIV.

I was taken aback. During the past 24 hours I had never thought, not even once that I might have the disease myself. Despite knowing a lot about AIDS, I was so shocked and overwhelmed with Carl's diagnosis and trying to help him through his ordeal that it had not occurred to me. I thought we had reached the pinnacle of disaster only to be jolted by Dr Grace's request.

Carl began to cry. Dr Grace had tears in her eyes. I was trying hard to stop my own tears.

On our way home, Carl shook his head saying, 'This I cannot take. Rose, if your test results are positive I cannot live through this.'

'But, you will have to.'

'I always thought that I was mentally strong and could even go to prison and be locked up for something that I didn't do. I think I could survive that, but not this.'

'Carl, you have to promise me that you will stop thinking like that. There are some positives. I am not sick. I have no symptoms. This means I am well enough to help and look after you. It could be worse. Both of us could be ill and unable to help each other. Even if my test results turn out to be positive, let's hope that I don't get sick for a long time.'

'Oh my God, the children, what are we going to do about them? What have I done?'

'What you cannot do is compound their loss any more

by thinking about suicide.'

'But how could I live with myself, knowing that I have given you a disease that might kill you?'

'I don't know how you are going to do it, but you have to. I am going to give you a very good reason: the children. Remember them. We went looking for them. These are children of our hearts. We owe it to them to do everything in our power, under the circumstances, to live as long as we can.'

'I can't believe that I have messed up my children's lives so badly.'

'And it can be worse if you won't stop contemplating suicide; the worse thing you could do in these circumstances.'

'I know Rose, but I can't shake the feeling of hopelessness and doom.'

That weekend I called on Carl's friend, Dr Winty, and told him that I thought that Carl was contemplating suicide. I told him that Carl had got himself into a state over the cancer diagnosis. Dr Winty came immediately, stayed for hours talking to Carl and did not leave until he thought that Carl was in a better state of mind. He encouraged Carl by discussing projects that they would do together in the future, in particular one on drug abuse in Jamaica. In fact, Carl spent a lot of time on this project in 1992.

The following Friday, Carl and I walked into Dr Grace's office and she told me immediately, 'I am sorry Mrs Stone, your tests are positive.'

A shiver ran through my whole body and tears began to stream down my face. Carl bent his head to his knees and I heard him sobbing.

Dr Grace talked to us as she usually did, in soft comforting tones. She tried to reassure us that she would do her best to ensure that we got all the benefit of her expertise together with what medicine had to offer. I tried to stop the flow of my tears but there seemed no end to them. At the very least, I had to stem the tears so that I could think clearly.

Carl, through his indiscretions, had brought me into this new family of people infected with and living with HIV/AIDS. I had to protect Tricia and Timothy from what Carl was feeling at that moment. He was guilt ridden and could only think that he did not deserve to live, especially because he had infected me. I had to suspend all my confused feelings over being infected by Carl for a while, at least until he achieved some perspective that he could live with. I had to believe that I could use the love that he had for the children to counterbalance his self-destructive thoughts. I knew that his friend Dr Winty would continue to help us.

The last 72 hours had put me in crisis mode, without time to reflect or plan. I was totally reactive. My friend Norma had given me a journal. She thought that I should write a daily account of what I was going through. I was not ready to write 'truths' in this journal and I was also fearful of someone reading it, but I did make one entry on Friday after we came back from the doctor.

Journal Entry

I don't know where my generosity of sprit comes from, but I know I have it in abundance. It is possible that I understand too much about human frailties and the compelling nature of these frailties. Therefore, right at this moment, early days yet, I am not assigning blame. I could easily say his lifestyle contributed to his becoming seriously ill. I could also say he should have checked with the doctor sooner, he should have done those tests that Dr Charles had ordered. I suppose I have said these things many times over and over again to him in our many years of marriage. I cannot say them now to him. I will not say them now because firstly I will not be the cause of any pain. He is suffering too much guilt and remorse. I am trying not to make him focus on these because these emotions are damaging to the human psyche.

I married Carl because I was passionately in love with him. I don't know how many friends and family understand that. I have had a fulfilling life with him even though he has been a difficult man to live with. I have always understood him and that has made life with him satisfying and comfortable, despite my ranting and raving.

LIKKLE PEPPA BUN BIG MAN MOUT

A seemingly minor indiscretion can result in a major disaster

IN THESE EARLY DAYS AFTER HIS DIAGNOSIS, Carl made weekly visits to see Dr Grace at her office at Medical Associates. I accompanied him and sat with him in the waiting area until she was ready for him. There were many times while in the waiting area Carl would sit with his head on my shoulder, because he was feeling physically ill or psychologically downtrodden. Later he would come out of her office with a smile on his face, seemingly less troubled than before. There was a task, however, that Carl had a difficult time completing. The Ministry of Health required that anyone who was infected with HIV gives the authorities the names, and if possible the addresses, of all their sexual partners for the last couple of years.

He eventually gave Dr Grace his list of ladies.

The next day, Saturday, I asked Norma to accompany me to the Manor Park Pharmacy. I had got myself fixated on buying new toothbrushes for the whole family. Dr Grace had mentioned that sometimes husbands and wives knowingly or unknowingly use each other's toothbrushes. I decided to buy distinctive colours so that there would be no likelihood of a mix-up. As soon as I started to choose the colours for Tricia and Timothy I felt myself getting a little out of control.

I could not decide what four colours to choose, I did not know how many to buy, I could not recall if the children used medium or soft bristles. The result of all my confusion is that I started taking up toothbrushes and putting them back at a frenzied pace. Norma tried to help me but I would not allow her to do so. Norma talked to me in soft tones but I was oblivious to her. At some point I realized that I was unable to buy the toothbrushes so I walked quickly from the pharmacy to my car only to burst out in tears. Norma bought the brushes for me and returned to the car.

'Rose, you will soon feel better.'

'I made a fool of myself. Is this what my life is going to be like now? I cannot make a simple decision.'

'You have to give yourself time to get used to all the things that are being thrown at you, all the new developments in your life.'

Norma, do you think it is unreasonable of me to expect that I can go in a pharmacy and buy four toothbrushes?'

'With all that you have made me privy to, if I were you I do not know if I would be standing at all. I might be in bed for a while. It has just been a month – give yourself time and allow your friends to help you.'

'If I thought that I was going to be confused, crushed and humiliated buying these items, I would have asked you to help and not enter the pharmacy at all. My thought processes were so extreme I actually thought that if I bought too many brushes everyone in the store would know I have HIV. The converse of that I felt too: that my family would surely suffer if I did not buy these toothbrushes tonight. I wonder if I am losing my mind.'

'I don't think so. You are still analysing your thoughts and actions in a rational way, so you are OK Rose. The stress is great, so do not minimize it in any way.'

'While I was crying and waiting for you I remembered a book that I had studied and taught in school. *Things Fall Apart* by Chinua Achebe. One of the main theses of this book is that when the Europeans went to Africa and began to systematically remove from the African societies their customs, their religion, everything that was familiar; in fact their way of life, things fell apart in most of these African countries.'

'I remember that book well.'

'I feel my whole family is falling apart and I do not know how to prevent it from happening. I am powerless. The irony is that as far as I am concerned, the part I played in allowing outside elements to destroy the foundations of this family was minimal but I now have to play a major role in trying to salvage what I can from the wreckage of infidelity and HIV/AIDS. I don't know after this display tonight if I even have the tools to attempt this.'

'I have faith in your abilities to hold the pieces together until you figure out what is to be done next. Give yourself time to work things out. I think you should give yourself a little credit for surviving this onslaught.'

'I have survived because I have lied to a lot of family and friends.'

'Let us leave that discussion for another time your husband must be looking for you by now.'

A couple of days later Carl provided for me the perfect segue that I needed for us to begin the dialogue about the rest of our lives together. As I entered our bedroom, he asked, 'Rose you forgot to wear your wedding band today.' I was amazed that Carl noticed the omission and was uncertain how to respond. I had not worn my wedding ring since his diagnosis.

'I did not forget I have not worn it for a while.'

'Does this mean that you will never wear it again?'

'It might, but symbolism is not something that should be high on our priority list of issues to talk about. I noticed that you gave Dr Grace the list of women that the authorities required. I want to discuss that...'

'Oh no, Rose please don't. It will be difficult on both of us and put further strain on our marriage.'

'Our what? Our *marriage?* You are making light of a serious matter, aren't you?!' I start to laugh as I often did at the most serious and inopportune times.

'Rose, you are not laughing at me, are you?' As I sat in the chair and looked at him facing me from the bed, I thought that I was going to need many more laughs to survive our ordeal.

'I wish my laughter could solve all our problems – so that when I am finished laughing, you would not have committed adultery and then spiced it up with some HIV that is eventually going to kill both of us.'

'I am so sorry, you have to know that it was not intentional. I thought I was always very careful.'

'I cannot believe I am discussing your infidelity with you. Carl, you have to understand that it is very painful for me, but since this is my reality I have to ask some questions. We have discussed our marriage many times and you have always said to me that you were content, satisfied and a very happy married man. You claimed to have no problems with the marriage. How do you square that with your list of names?'

'Do you think this is the right time to be examining these matters Rose? No matter what you think, I am worried about you. I don't want to be the cause of any more pain than is absolutely necessary.'

'Forget about the pain part. You have cornered that market. All the pain that I am having or will ever have in my life will in some way be connected to you. Answer the question.'

'That's so harsh, I cannot do this.'

'Try. You have to.'

Carl got up and walked around the room. 'I have been very happy and contented with you. Our marriage works on so many levels.'

'So how come there is a list that I have to contend with?'

'Rose, you know that my infidelity has nothing to do with you or the state of the marriage.'

'That's bulls---! You cannot be having the women and the good marriage "that works on so many levels" and truly believe that that kind of living, apart from being schizophrenic, won't have repercussions.'

'To be truthful Rose, the worst thing that I thought could have been an outcome would be that you would find out and I could lose you.'

'Forget about me – what about you? Was it not more difficult to design your life around these two entities than just one? Was it pure machismo that allowed your mind and body to cheat, knowing that your losing your whole family was at stake?'

'I do not have the answers to your questions. These are

questions that I am not sure can be answered; they are complex. And no matter what the circumstance and regardless of what you say, I will not say anything that will hurt you further.'

'That's a cop out.'

'Yes, it is, I plead guilty.'

'Anyway, back to the list…'

'You are not going to ask me to give you the names are you?'

'No, I already have a list in my head that goes back to the beginning of our marriage. I don't need any additional information that I am certainly not emotionally ready to handle.'

'Rose, I am begging you to reconsider the whole line of questioning. You are crying and getting more upset. I am going downstairs to get something for both of us to drink. Is that all right?'

'Yes, but don't stay too long.'

As Carl's footsteps retreat down the stairs, I wondered if what I was attempting to do was futile. I knew I needed to have this conversation with Carl so that I could put the anger and pain that I was feeling into some kind of perspective. Yet even as I thought this it seemed nonsensical. There was no way to rationalize my feelings over the destruction of a 20-year relationship, especially in one afternoon. My instincts told me that I had to find someplace in my mind, where hurt could reside, if only for a while. I was beginning to feel resentment for having to nurse Carl through an illness that was as a result of infidelity. I could not function like this. My own self-preservation depended on how I resolved this within me. As soon as Carl had returned and I had sipped a little of the water he had brought me, I resumed questioning him.

'Has it crossed your mind that I might leave you?'

'Every minute. Every second of the day.'

'Why do you think I am still here?'

'There you go again asking me impossible questions.'

'Why not hazard a guess. You can't get into any more trouble with your answers.'

'At this stage I believe I can. Seriously Rose, I think the children are a part of it, secondly the love we have for each other and lastly you have a lot of compassion for me, you feel sorry for me.'

'I never thought of leaving under these circumstances. I need some honesty from you in order to quiet my personal misgivings for staying. No matter how painful you think it is for me, you have to give me the information.'

'Rose, please don't.'

'Over the years I have accused or hinted that there are women I know of that I think you have had relations with which you have vehemently denied. I am going to call some names and all that is required of you is a simple yes or no. I will try to be satisfied with that.'

Carl started to pace the room.

'I feel cornered…'

'I have finished debating. I am going to begin now, Mary…'

I closed my eyes and recited names from memory and listened while Carl answered yes or no to each. Every time there was a positive response, my body jerked. I felt that I had received a physical blow. When my emotional hell was complete, I left Carl, went into the bathroom and locked the door.

I stepped into the bath, turned on the shower over my body and tried to breathe normally. Pain assaulted my mind and body. I had to hold on just to keep from falling. The water was warm, cold and warm again, but I allowed it to be a balm. I knew in those moments that normal life for me was in the past. Deprivation of all kinds was now my present and future. I cried loudly, I howled, I shouted, I sobbed and I moaned as I gave in to the most profound grief since finding out about AIDS.

After what seemed like hours of suffering, I turned off the tap. It had been only half an hour, but I had crossed a bridge between my physical reality and a way to deal with it mentally. I felt cleansed of the horror of Carl's infidelity and instead of choosing condemnation I chose forgiveness. For me there was no other route.

I had deceived all of my family and most of my friends. I had to find one place where I could maintain peace of mind and tranquillity, and that was inside my home. I needed to help Carl to live as long as possible. I needed to take our children through this journey, leaving them with as few scars as possible.

BULL HORN NEBBA TOO HEAVY FI BULL HEAD

There are some personal burdens in life, which must be carried because they are no one else's

THE DOCTORS CONTINUED TO BE AMAZED that Carl had been sick for so long and remained undiagnosed for at least five years. Carl marvelled at the amount of work that he produced over the same period. What I was more stupefied by, is that I had missed it all. I had failed to see that Carl had a real serious illness. In retrospect I realized that in 1989 we had gone to Europe and that Carl was not well on that trip. In June of that year we celebrated our fifteenth wedding anniversary. We were first planning to have a party and then decided against it. I thought that our marriage needed us to spend some time alone together, and that Carl needed to stop working so hard and to relax for at least two weeks.

When the trip was in the planning stage, Carl became lukewarm about it. He claimed that the timing was all wrong because he had deadlines to meet. I was upset and I made Carl know that. I told him he had the responsibility after this to plan the trip and furthermore, that he had to put on a smile when speaking of it. This he did under duress.

The seven-day bus tour through Europe stopped in Brussels, Belgium; Innsbrook, Austria; Lucerne, Switzerland; Rome and Florence, Italy; and Paris,

France. Our flight landed in London before the check-in time at the Royal National Hotel. Carl had to store our suitcases for a couple of hours in a designated area. The first sign of trouble was that after carrying our suitcases Carl was sweating profusely and seemed fatigued. We went into a small restaurant nearby to sit and talk. He could not explain why he was feeling badly, and furthermore, he said, he had a stomachache. We had to go to the pharmacy where we picked up some natural stomach remedies that the pharmacist recommended. Carl was feeling a little better the next day when we met Ian, our tour guide, and boarded the bus to take us to the ferry to Belgium. I was determined that no matter how Carl's face looked, how he said he felt, I was not going to allow him to spoil my enjoyment of this trip. I was excited to arrive in Belgium and I took part in all the activities that Ian had planned for our group. Carl slept through most of these. I was actually glad to see him sleep because I thought that he needed the rest.

When the bus was passing through Lucerne on our way to the hotel, I saw some lovely antique shops that I wanted to visit later, and Carl promised we would do so. Later, after walking hand in hand for ten minutes, on our way to these shops Carl said that he had suddenly felt unwell; his stomach was acting up again. I let go of his hand immediately. The shops were just five minutes away, I said. He replied that he felt really uncomfortable and wanted to return to the hotel. I took one look at him and left him at the side of the road, storming back to the hotel not looking back, not even once. I was very angry. Carl returned later and I had never seen him so upset with me in our whole marriage.

'Rose I can't believe that you left me on the roadside.' His voice was raised in anger and hurt.

'I can't believe you didn't go to the shops with me.'

'But I am not feeling well. What part of that don't you understand?'

'I don't believe you.'

'What? What do you mean you don't believe me?' His voice went up another octave.

'I believe your illnesses on this trip are very convenient.'

'What does that mean?'

I was sure that everyone on our floor (all the people on our tour) could hear Carl's voice.

'It means you get conveniently ill when we are going to do something that I want to do and you are quite fine at other times.'

'What are these other times that you are talking about?'

'No matter how sick you say you are during the day, we have made love every night since we are here and you are never ill during these times.'

'Rose, you astound me, you simply astound me. Do you believe I am faking feeling unwell?'

'Yes. I do. It is probably something psychological and it has been happening for some time now. Every time you have to go out with me you get ill or too tired.'

'That is utter rubbish. I don't know why I get ill during certain times of the day. I don't know why it lasts for a couple of hours and then the bad feelings go away. I have no control over these feelings. Rose, I stood and watched you walk away from me. I can't believe you did that to me.'

'I can't believe you did not go to the shops with me.'

'Rose, for the first time since I married you I have to question if you really love me. I can't believe you didn't look back. Suppose something further had happened to me? How could you do that? I cannot believe that you could love someone and do that to them.'

No matter what Carl did or said I was going to enjoy this tour through Europe. During the bus tour and the seven days after that which we spent in London, Carl looked distressed and uncomfortable. At the time I thought that these feelings were connected to the fact that he probably did not want to be travelling. And in fact, Carl continued to work during our two-week vacation. While travelling from Italy to France, he even tried to co-opt me. When Carl took out what seemed like reams of paper and handed them to me, I was completely stunned. Had he not understood that I was not going to allow him to spoil my vacation? I thought of just saying no, but decided against it and worked with him for about ten minutes. At that point I realized that I had to say something to him or else I would be working on Latin American poverty for another two hours.

'Carl, can you imagine when I go back to Jamaica and tell my friends that instead of enjoying the countryside, we were both working? If only my friends could see me now.'

Carl quickly took all the papers from me and put them back into his bag, but they reappeared a few days later in London. Carl continued to work and we continued to make love all during the 14 days of our vacation. It's little wonder, I suppose, that I failed to see his physical complaints then as symptoms of a serious illness. What it did ensure was that, even if I was not infected before, I would be now, even though there would be no way that either Carl or I could have known this in 1989.

After his diagnosis, Carl had many symptoms and they did not always appear together. Generally he seemed to be losing weight slowly but steadily. He looked gaunt, sometimes more so than others. There were times, however, when one symptom was so severe that we would all have to pay attention. He had high- and low-grade fevers, fungal infections, intestinal discomfort, suppressed appetite leading to weight loss and low haemoglobin count. The haemoglobin count was of great concern because it weakened his entire system. Between February and November of 1992, Carl had two blood transfusions at a private hospital. I told no one about these. He just spent the night there and came out in the morning. The transfusions usually revived him and made him feel better.

The doctors made the decision to put both of us on AZT, the only drug available for this disease at the time. I was HIV positive but not symptomatic. The only change that I felt physically was that I was always tired. I actually got up in the mornings feeling tired. I was not sure whether this was mental exhaustion, or the disease itself. Once I had begun taking the AZT, I was sick many times every day, so I had to take another drug to suppress the vomiting. Even then I vomited once a day, every day from March 1992 to June 1993, when the doctors decided to take me off this drug. All of this had to be hidden from my friends and family. I became an expert at being sick in plain sight; no one around me noticed that I was constantly sick. My only haven for my vomiting spells was Norma's house. Norma had been divorced for many years now and her children were grown and away at college. I would sometimes have to drive very fast from wherever I was to her house and she knew when I blew the horn in her carport that she was to quickly prepare for me.

Carl's body did not respond as poorly as mine to the taking of the AZT. He had no problems with it. For every symptom that Carl had, he had to be prescribed medication, which resulted in his taking several tablets daily. Yet in general, neither his system nor his psyche rebelled against it.

On Valentines Day 1992, our friend Dr Winty was putting on and singing in a concert at the Little Theatre. We all thought that it was a good idea to go. Carl and I took Tricia along with us. As it turned out, however, the concert was the worse thing for me. Hearing love songs and the whole joyful atmosphere made me feel, first, that I was a hypocrite, and second that this was not the right thing for me to do in order to protect my sanity.

I kept myself together during the concert, but afterwards, in the car on the way home when the radio started playing more love songs, my tears fell and I had no power to stop them. One of our favourites, one Carl and I used to dance to, 'Endless Love' by Lionel Ritchie and Diana Ross, started playing. Tricia was in the back and I didn't want her to know that I was crying. Fortunately, when her favourite, a Michael Jackson song began, she asked us to turn up the radio. Carl put his hand on my leg and tried his best to comfort me in an inconspicuous way, speaking quietly to me.

From March to December 1992 Carl was very ill and symptomatic. On March 23 of that year he made a presentation to The National Council on Drug Abuse Secretariat at the Jamaica Grande Resort entitled 'Values, Norms and Personality Development in Jamaica'. This paper proved to be important in the political life of Jamaica, and is still a vibrant part of the debate 14 years later. He conducted research for the Drug Abuse Secretariat, which led to a summer workshop, July 22 to 25, at the Americana Hotel in Ocho Rios. Carl's contribution to the workshop was a paper entitled 'Traditional versus Non-Traditional Methods of Communication in Contemporary Jamaica'. The participants in the workshop were community leaders drawn from the Community-based Development Action Committee (CODAC) and treatment centres of six specified communities. In October 1992, a three-day International conference on Drug Abuse was held at the Jamaica Conference Centre. Carl gave a report on the Drug Abuse studies he had done in Jamaica and discussed the implications for the future. He continued to accept speaking engagements and spoke at the Grace Kennedy Awards Ceremony at the Devonshire Restaurant at Devon House.

In trying to record the events of that fateful year, January 1992 to February 1993, I see it as one long nightmare. But I know it was made up of everyday occurrences and crises. There were days when the stress seemed unbearable for me. I understood that Carl needed more attention than ever simply because he was ill, but it was extremely difficult for me during the summer months when school was out. One evening when I returned home the children met me in distress complaining, 'Daddy wants you. Daddy has been trying to get you everywhere.' I ran into the office and saw Carl working at the computer.

'Are you ill, is this an emergency?'

'No, why?'

'The children told me that you were inquiring about my whereabouts and phoning and trying to find out where I was.'

'Rose, I can be worried about you, can't I?'

'Carl, you have been doing this "search-for-me thing," for some time now and I don't like it, especially under the circumstances we find ourselves in.'

'Why is it such a big thing that I want to know where you are?'

'Do you think I am seeing a man?'

'I don't even know how to answer that.'

'Well, I will answer it for you. No, No and No. Remember that your actions during our marriage have sealed my fate when it comes to men. Not only will no one want to be involved with someone with HIV, but certainly you have showed me how unevenly balanced the relationship between a man and a woman is. I went into the relationship with you, I thought on par, but men have the upper hand every time. I feel so much at a disadvantage now that you don't have to worry about me getting into any relationship with anyone.'

'Rose, that is a little harsh and my trying to find out where you were had nothing to do with that. I was just worried and wanted to see if you were OK.'

'Carl, whenever I am "missing", I am at Norma's. I only go up there when you are not in crisis. Please don't call me or make the children call me unless it is an emergency. I have told you that you have to find someone else besides me to talk to. You are doing what your mother tried to do to me. I told her then that she needed a friend and I am telling you now, you have to find someone to talk to.'

'So now you are prescribing for my social and mental needs?'

'No, but on second thought, can't you find one friend out of all the women you have had, to talk to? You must have made one friend.'

'Rose, what are you saying really? Are you listening to yourself?'

'I am saying to you that I am giving you permission, if that is what you need, to find a friend to talk to, among all the women you have had, because I cannot manage this constant need you have for me. I actually feel demeaned by it. There was a time when there was nothing else that would have pleased me more than my husband wanting to be with me constantly. Certainly, I don't feel that way any more. Even though my heart is breaking in two for you and what you have to go through I cannot be responsible for this part of your needs.'

'Rose, I am so sorry to have put you through all this. I

promise that I won't call you up at Norma's. Regardless of what you think of me, you are the only friend that I need now.'

Carl returned to lecturing at the university, but he encountered an assortment of physical problems from day to day. This usually occurred in the evening or on his way home from the university or from picking up the children from school or dancing or music lessons. During this period Carl did not feel hungry often and he was not keeping his food down well. One particular day while returning from the university he felt for some soup. He stopped, bought it and ate it at a restaurant in the Liguanea area. By the time he reached home, though, all that he consumed was now on his clothing and the floor of the car. I was glad the children were not there to see this and I quickly dealt with cleaning up Carl and the car as I had done so many times before. There was another day, however, when Carl came home smiling.

'Rose I had a very rewarding experience. I felt that I was given a gift today. I know now why I love teaching so much.'

'So what happened?'

'When I entered the lecture room, I started to feel sick. I felt like my head was spinning but I wanted to give the lecture anyway.'

'Couldn't you have put off the lecture?'

'It was too late and I was already in the classroom and the students were all there. So I told the students that I was not feeling well and I was going to rest for a while.

I just sat down and rested my head on the desk. Rose, I don't know how long I was there, but it must have been about ten to fifteen minutes. What was so fantastic, Rose, was when I raised my head and stood up, all the students were still there, not one of them had left. I could not believe that. At the end of the lecture all the students gave me a standing ovation.'

Carl came to me and hugged me, and as he did he was his old self again, happy, smiling and relaxed. I wondered if we would ever receive another moment like this.

In November 1992 the department of government at the university in conjunction with the faculty of social sciences hosted a two-day conference to explore the different dimensions of Carl's efforts and his contributions. Each of the nine sessions represented a facet of Carl's work. The nearly 50 participants represented a wide cross section of the society, including community leaders, trade unionists, politicians, private sector leaders and academics. Dr Carlton Davis, then Executive Chairman of the Jamaica Bauxite Institute, gave the keynote address. As part of this effort, Carl was also a guest on the television programme, *Profile* which then aired on Sundays on the Jamaica Broadcasting Corporation (JBC) television station. The week of activities also included a dinner at the Terra Nova Hotel.

On the television feature Carl spoke about death. He said he was not afraid to die and that death had no special terrors for him. We had talked together about dying and I believed him when he said that. Earlier on in this fateful year, I had sometimes walked with him at the Mona dam where we discussed a wide array of topics which were both general and personal. Those early morning talks represented a continuation of the dialogue between Carl and me that started when we met. While I thoroughly enjoyed these talks and was grateful for the opportunity to be able to have them, they were bittersweet for me as I realized that it would, more than likely, be the last time that we would be speaking about these things. Added to this, there were topics that Carl felt more freedom to share with me in my dual role as wife and friend. This was not always easy for me to take.

As Carl's wife, and his caregiver, I was concerned about the effect of these functions on his health. But Carl enjoyed them so much, especially the conference. He told me later that it was rewarding to see all his hard work touch so many areas of public life, and he appreciated the papers and the commentary on his work. Carl attended all nine sessions of the conference. Some of his colleagues even remarked on how well he looked. To say that I was nervous would be an understatement. I attended as many sessions as I could and I was there for the final day, which was an open session where the audience participated by giving views and suggestions. Paul Ashley, a specially invited guest, voiced the sentiment that the newly constructed hall should be named after Carl to honour his work and contribution to Jamaica. Christine Cummings of the Department of Government coordinated this whole effort, including the dinner at Terra Nova Hotel. I had a very hard time making up the list of family and friends to be invited. When I finally handed it to Christine, I shared with her that I felt as if I was inviting people to Carl's funeral. Her response was comforting, but I really felt that physically I could not bear to attend the Terra Nova dinner and listen to Carl make his last speech. It was only with Dr Matt's advice and support that I was able to make it through this whole ordeal. Dr Matt was my children's paediatrician and, throughout Carl's illness, had become a friend.

The details of the Terra Nova dinner are lost to me. I remember being stressed beyond my capacity. Most of my thoughts were centred on Carl and whether he would be able to get through the evening. I did not want to be there. I did not want Carl to be there. A huge part of my self-inflicted stress was that when I looked around the room, I saw friends, family and colleagues of Carl, all of whom I had directly or indirectly lied to. The night could not go by quickly enough for me. When the dinner ended I tried to get Carl to leave quickly but that was an impossible task, as everyone wanted to speak with him. While my memory of the evening is still fuzzy, the anguish I felt, I can touch even now.

In December, Carl started correcting university scripts for final examinations. He had always been proud of his efficiency in correcting scripts. As his physical state deteriorated, however, this ability was compromised. We spoke about this and I reminded him of the alternative of allowing his colleagues in the department of government to correct the scripts for him. He decided to give himself a couple of days to see if he would feel well enough to do it himself. In the interim I called the Department of Government and alerted them that Carl might not be able to complete marking his scripts. I gently prodded Carl into not expending what energy he had on something that others could do for him.

Carl finally relented, and Dr Trevor Munroe came and collected the scripts from him. They chatted for a couple of minutes, and I felt the pain of what this turning point meant to Carl. He told me later that giving back the scripts represented for him the first time in his life he had been unable to keep a deadline. I tried my best to comfort him.

Pearnel Charles, a member of the JLP opposition party, was among the many people who telephoned Carl during December. Pearnel was concerned that in the 20-odd years that he had known Carl, this was the first time that Carl mentioned being tired. He offered to arrange a two-night stay at the Sandals Dunns River. We decided to accept, and to combine this stay at Sandals with a visit to Leroy and his family who were on their annual vacation in Mamee Bay, close to the hotel. As we drove together to Mamee Bay with Tricia and Timothy, I could see that they were upset not only because they were not accompanying us to Sandals, but because Carl got sick a few times on the way. After a short visit with Carl's family, I left behind two children who would rather have come along with their parents than stay with their grandmother and uncle, and bewildered-looking in-laws, and we made our way to Sandals.

Carl wanted the weekend to be as normal as possible.

He insisted on going down to breakfast with all the other guests. I could see how deliberate he was while having his fruits and how slowly he chewed and swallowed each mouthful. I knew he was trying his best to ensure that everything he ate remained in his stomach. After breakfast I suggested to Carl that we remain seated for a while so as to achieve this. We talked, we laughed; other guests joined us for short two-to five-minute chats, and workers, including management, came to talk to Carl. Before we knew it, two and a half hours had passed since we began breakfast. Carl assured me that his stomach was no longer queasy, so we got up and made our way back to our room.

As we were passing the table tennis boards Carl suggested that we play a game. This was a bad idea, for me psychologically and him physically. I realized that he was just trying to do something that he knew that I would like to do, and I had a hard time not showing emotional resentment to this idea. In the past, when he was healthy, I sometimes had to bribe him to play table tennis with me. As I looked across on Carl's frail body holding the table tennis ball and racket, my only consolation was that he probably knew what my thoughts were.

'Carl I don't think this is a good idea. You might get sick and then it would defeat the whole purpose of our sitting two and a half hours for breakfast.'

'I am OK, Rose, please play with me just for a short while.'

As we played, I kept retrieving balls on my side of

the table as well as on his side. Carl became visibly weaker, and the game became sadder and sadder as the minutes ticked by. A tennis game between Carl and me at this time was distressing even as a concept. The actual game itself was miserable and to have our play end so soon after it started, and to walk away from the game was upsetting. Carl clutched my hand and said, 'Rose I am so sorry.' I continued to hold all my emotions below the surface and said, 'I just hope your breakfast stays down.'

A normal weekend it was not. Carl seemed to get frailer as time went on. To underscore this, when we were ready to leave the hotel I asked Carl if he would like me to call the bellhop to take our bags downstairs. For the first time in our marriage he allowed someone to carry our luggage.

Traditionally for Carl and me, New Year's Eve was a time when we would get together with friends and party, but it was impossible for me to feel festive when he was looking and feeling so rotten. Still, Carl wanted the four of us to go out together. I was hesitant, but as a result of Carl's insistence that the whole family go out together, and Tricia and Timothy's glee over spending New Year's Eve with us, we all dressed up and went to Maureen, the usual gathering spot for our group of friends for at least the past five years. We visited for a while took some photographs and then went on to Dr Winty's party where we greeted friends, ate, sat down and chatted, and then left.

As I drove home that New Year's Eve before midnight, I could not help recalling that just a little over a year ago, the four of us had dressed and gone to a Third World concert, not realizing that it would mark the beginning of a new era in our lives.

January 1993

Carl continued to write his biweekly column for the *Gleaner*. His mind was as sharp as ever, though his physical capabilities were deteriorating. Towards the middle of January he had written a column on his computer at home and instead of touching the key to save, he touched the one to erase. He was completely distraught and exhausted when he phoned me. I felt compelled to help him. This person sitting before me was in sharp contrast to the vibrant, virile man that I had fallen in love with and married. The empathy that I felt for him overwhelmed me. The dilemma facing us was that Carl thought that this was a very good column, and he desperately wanted to record and publish it. He knew not only that I hated typing but that I was not a competent typist. Nevertheless, I spent the next three hours typing and in the end Carl published his column.

A couple of days later when Carl was in the family room listening to music, I came to ask him what he wanted for supper. Unbelievably he asked me to dance with him.

'But you can't dance, Carl.'

'Rose, please dance with me.'

Many thoughts entered my mind, the kindest of which was that he was always too busy to dance. Perhaps because he held out his hand to me or perhaps because I did not want to deal with all the other ugly thoughts in my head, I decided to step into his arms. I was ill at ease there and as usual Carl knew that.

'Carl you do not have to do this,' I said.

'I know. I know.' He whispered in my ear, 'I know what you are thinking. You are thinking of all the other times when you wanted to dance and I thought of it as frivolity. And now that I can barely move my feet I want to dance with you. I am so sorry Rose, I have gotten it. All that you were trying to show me, I have gotten it, even if it seems too late to you.'

Tears began to fall down my face uncontrollably; tears of regret and sorrow. Carl hugged me for as long as he could.

When the new term started for Tricia and Timothy, Carl was still taking them to school in the mornings. As with the scripts, however, we had talked earlier about not doing this task. I knew that Carl would not be able to do it for much longer. In early February after returning home, he told me that he had dropped them for the last time that day.

'What happened?' I asked.

'I couldn't negotiate a turn properly when I was dropping Tricia to St. Hugh's.'

'Did you say anything to the children?'

'Yes, I did. I reminded them that I had been ill for a long time and that I would not be able to drive them to school any more because I was feeling very weak. Timothy asked me who would take them to school and I told him that for a time probably Mommy would and that if Mommy couldn't do it they would have to take the bus. I also told them that if anything happened to me, they were to help their Mommy out as much as possible. I told them about the money I had in the bank that was to be used for their needs. I reminded Tricia that since she was the older one she was to stay close to you and help you out as much as possible.'

'Do you think they understood everything?'

'I am not so sure. I know they were a little upset and surprised that I had a hard time with the turn at the school gate. I hope that even if they don't understand it now, they will remember it for the future.'

'When I take them to school in the morning I will talk to them again,' I said. 'I'll see what they have absorbed and try to reinforce what I can.'

The following day I did just that.

'Did Daddy talk to you about his illness yesterday?' Tricia was quick to answer.

'Mommy, Daddy couldn't find the gate.'

'Which gate?'

'My school gate. He had to reverse many times before he could turn in.'

'What do you think happened to him?'

'He was weak. He said he could not take us to school anymore. At least he is not as sick as when we were going to the country. Mommy, remember he brought up a lot of green stuff.'

'Yuck,' Timothy interjected. 'Daddy was really, really sick.'

'Your Daddy is very, very sick now. Even though you don't see him vomiting he is still sick and might not get better.'

'He is still doing work on the computer. Tricia, didn't you see Daddy working on the computer yesterday?'

'Yes, Timothy. He probably is feeling better.'

'Tricia and Timothy, listen very carefully to Mommy. The disease that Daddy has caused him to be very ill and he might not get better. He might have to leave us.'

'Mommy, are you saying that Daddy is going to die soon?'

'Tricia, I don't know when Daddy is going to die. But what I do know is that we all have to prepare ourselves for that. Let us get back to what I said earlier. Timothy, what do you remember Daddy saying to you yesterday?'

'I remember him telling us he can't take us to school any longer because he can't drive the car.'

'And what do you remember Tricia?'

'He told us we might have to take the bus and that we don't have to worry about money because he has lots and lots of money in the bank.'

'You both have to remember that Daddy and I love you very much and if bad things happen, you will always have my family and friends to take care of you. Remember, if you have any questions, come and ask me. And you can ask Daddy too about how he is feeling.'

As I dropped off the children that morning in early February 1993, reality hit me squarely in the face. *Carl is going to die soon. I don't think he will live out 1993. I will have to deal with his death and the circumstances surrounding it. Will I be strong enough both mentally and physically to cope with all of this? I don't know if he is going to have a long illness or if he is going to die suddenly. I will have to talk with my friends, Shelly, Norma and John about this, so that I can prepare myself.*

The very next morning when I was about to take the children to school I noticed that we had a flat tyre. Timothy ran upstairs to tell his father. I turned to Tricia and asked, 'Do you think that Dumpling from down the street will change it for us?' When I went inside, Carl was coming down the stairs with Timothy.

'Carl I have asked Dumpling to change the tyre for us – do you think it is a good idea?'

'Yes Rose, I think so.' He put his hand on Timothy's head and rubbed it.

'Daddy is not feeling so well today Timmy, so Dumpling will change the tyre for us.'

IF PLAANTN BEN KNOW SEH 'IM NEK GWINE BRUK, 'IM NEBBA WOULDA SHOOT

If people knew how dearly they would pay for getting involved in certain situations, they would avoid them

JANUARY 1993. It had been one year since Carl's diagnosis, and my whole life since then had been consumed with keeping him alive. At first it meant weekly visits to Dr Grace. Then we graduated to bimonthly visits. By late January we were visiting once per month. I spoke to Dr Grace and Dr Barry almost daily, and Dr Matt weekly. There was hardly any time for reflection. And there was no planning, only responding to each crisis. Twice Carl's haemoglobin count fell below the normal level and he had to be hospitalized to receive blood transfusions. Numerous tests were done and medication given that year to clear up bacterial or fungal infections. It was not unusual for me to call Dr Grace between visits and tell her something had gone wrong.

That same Monday when Carl had conceded that he could not change the tyre on the car, I started noticing that he had looked a little different – in a way that I could not explain. He did not have a good Monday night; he was in a great deal of discomfort and hardly slept. When I called the doctor on Tuesday morning and explained she said that we should come right away to the Blood Bank for a visit. After examining Carl, Dr Grace told me that he was completely dehydrated and would have to be hospitalized. She could not explain why he had become dehydrated so quickly so she needed to run some tests. I felt a stab of apprehension.

Carl was hooked up to IV needles and in the Medical Centre for two days when Dr Grace called me to talk to me about the test results. I had not told any family members about the hospitalization. My closest allies at the time, Shelly, Norma and John, were the only ones who knew. I had hoped it would be a short stay so that I could get away without saying anything to anyone else.

As Dr Grace and I sat on the bench outside the ward in the lobby she began, 'The results are back and they are not very good.'

'What does that mean?'

'It means that your husband is very, very ill.'

'Is this the kind of "ill" for which I call his 87-year-old mother and tell her that he is in the hospital and that she should visit?'

'Yes, you have to do that immediately.' I tried to absorb this new information.

'OK, I will.'

'Professor Stone and I have talked and he had requested that he not be kept in the hospital on any life-support systems. Are you still OK with that?'

'Yes … Yes.'

The dark feelings that I had tried to keep in the realms of imagination and nightmare were finally with me, infusing my body with dread.

'So essentially what I am doing is giving him lots of fluids and vitamins and preparing him for you to take him home,' said the doctor. 'I am so sorry Mrs Stone. The kidney function is way down and your husband might go into renal failure soon.'

'How are you going to tell him this?'

'Come in with me and just follow my lead. I am going to tell him now.'

As we entered Carl's room, he greeted the doctor smiling, and said, 'It's all over for me Doc, isn't it?'

'The test results are not good at all, Professor. Your kidneys seem to be shutting down on you, but I am going to fix you up and send you home, and over the weekend I am going to consult with some other colleagues and see what else we can come up with. So I'll come and see you on Monday and we can talk further.'

'So when can I leave hospital?'

Before giving her a chance to respond I asked in disbelief 'Consult with some colleagues?'

Dr Grace looked at me and immediately I understood. 'Professor Stone, we will try to get everything on stream and we will try to get you out by Saturday morning. Is that OK?'

'Yes Doc.'

That evening Mother, and her friend Mrs Lyn Chamberlain came to visit Carl at the Medical Centre, but I stayed with Carl, as I usually did, long after visiting hours were over. I remember remarking to him how differently some of the nurses behaved towards us in front of the doctors compared to the way they behaved when the doctors were not there. When the doctors were present the nurses behaved professionally. However, when the doctors were not there some nurses made their displeasure at having to treat Carl very apparent. That night was a prefect example of this.

Carl wanted to go to the bathroom, so he pressed the buzzer to call the nurse. After waiting a while he pressed again. I volunteered to go and call a nurse, but Carl did not want me to leave him. Instead I went into the bathroom to get the bedpan. I did not see one. By the time I came back and pressed the buzzer for the third time Carl had started to raise himself up.

'Carl, I don't think that this is a good idea.'

'Its OK, you just help me off the bed.'

'Dr Grace said you were to remain in bed.'

'But I want to use the bathroom – and don't you see that nobody is coming.'

'I will try to help you but you are so weak and I am weak too.'

As I struggled to help Carl off the bed, with him attached to and holding and pulling his IV equipment, I put one arm around him to support his frail body. The bathroom was just a few feet from us but it seemed like a football field away. We slipped and we slid but we remained upright. I hoped a nurse would get here soon because I was afraid that Carl was going to fall and hurt himself. As we reached the vicinity of the bathroom Carl did fall, and I went down with him. The IV pole ended up askew. While attempting to get up from the floor, I sensed a presence, glanced up at the glass panel door and saw a nurse looking directly at us. I was grateful that she was there and for a split second I looked away to help Carl get up. By the time I glanced back she was nowhere to be seen.

'Rose, was someone at the door?'

'No Carl.'

'Are you sure?'

'Yes Carl, there was no one.'

My eyes were filled with tears that I did not want him to see. We somehow managed to get up, reach the bathroom and return him to the bed. It seemed to take hours. The struggle was physically and emotionally draining and had been made all the worse by the nurse's unprofessional conduct and lack of compassion.

By February 13, 1993, the day that Carl left the Medical Centre to come home, I had been able to tell both sides of the family and friends that Carl's kidneys were failing. My sister Andrea came to stay and support me, and she has been with me ever since. My brother Barry was also at my home that morning and was able to assist Carl upstairs. Barry was shocked to see how Carl had deteriorated in such a short time. When Carl came upstairs he first walked through the bedrooms and family room over and over again, stopping in both Tricia and Timothy's bedrooms, staring at walls and looking in their closets. It took me a long time to settle him in our bedroom that day.

After his return home, every day presented a new hurdle. There were challenges surrounding his lack of sleep, his restlessness, his agitation and his lack of appetite. John suggested to me that I would be better able to look after Carl if he was in a hospital bed. Dr Winty and Dr Grace concurred. Dr Winty gave me some ideas as to where and how I could obtain one. The department of government and Dr Don Robotham from the faculty of social sciences used their influence with the University Hospital to secure a bed for us.

When it arrived however, Carl would not use it immediately. I tried to cajole him into lying in the bed for even short periods but as in so many other things, he told me he would go when he needed it.

The editor of the *Gleaner* at the time called me to find out how Carl was. He asked about a poll that Carl was doing and what stage the work had reached. I told him that the interviewers had collected the data and that I was in possession of it. Was there any way I could finish the poll so that they could publish it? he asked. I told him I did not think so because I have never had to do a poll on my own. Would I think about it? He would call back the next day.

I mentioned this conversation to Carl and he encouraged me to do as the editor requested. Over the next few days, he walked me through the poll.

On a daily basis I faced the challenge of answering numerous phone calls from all over the world and handling the volume of family, friends and colleagues who came to see Carl. When you join your life with that of your loved one, you do not contemplate a period such as this: preparing for his death. My only comfort during this time was the love and support of family and friends.

Carl's 89-year-old Aunt G, called me regularly from Florida over this period. As a nurse, she understood a lot of what Carl was going through and so she was able to empathize and offer good advice. She was also helpful in quelling my fears about Mother's ability to cope with the impending death of her son. During one of these conversations, I mentioned that Mother's behaviour towards me had been unfriendly which was uncharacteristic of her.

'Rose, don't worry about Flo. She is very strong and she will get through this. From the time we were growing up, Rose, when she is under stress she acts up but don't worry, she is stronger than all of us put together.'

'Reverend Thompson came to see Carl the other day and Mother told me after he left that she was spending the night because her priest gave her permission to do so. Which she proceeded to do.'

'But how could he give her permission to stay the night at your house?'

'I don't think he would have done that, but that's how Mother presented it. How am I supposed to cope with her as well as with Carl and the children?'

'Don't allow Flo to make you upset and keep you from doing the best for Carl. The important person is Carl.'

'What I was afraid of, Aunt G, is that she would have gotten sick. Carl is already sick in the house. I can't manage anyone else being ill.'

'She is not going to get sick.'

'But how can you be sure…'

'I will talk to her tomorrow and I will also talk to Leroy because Leroy knows his mother and can handle her. In any case he will soon come down and take her off your hands.'

Aunt G and I had always gotten along well and I was relieved that she was able to understand how these seemingly small matters could overwhelm my already crammed mind.

The daunting part for me personally was to have Carl's deterioration witnessed by his colleagues, people he had worked with over the years and of course the politicians. Carl was a political scientist, and he had personal and professional relationships on both sides of the political divide. The People's National Party (PNP) formed the government at the time. Some members of the government, Carl had great respect for; others he had mentored; some barely tolerated him, and he them.

One of the rules I made to help me to cope was that I would not turn down anyone who wanted to come to the house to visit, on the understanding that they might not be able to see Carl if he was not feeling well enough that day. Consequently, many people who came remained downstairs and just visited with me, his mother or whoever else was there at the time. The prime minister; P.J. Patterson, Mr. Hugh Shearer, Miss Portia Simpson and Carl's personal friend Cliff Stone were among many politicians who visited me, offered words of encouragement and even brought me flowers.

Towards the end of the first week after Carl came home, the leader of the opposition, Mr Edward Seaga, paid a visit. I knew that Carl liked Mr Seaga and had a great deal of respect for him as a politician and a person. Mr Seaga's request to go upstairs and see Carl seemed strange to me as I had explained that Carl was weak and speaking in low tones that would make conversation difficult. Mr Seaga said that was okay and went on up to the bedroom for what seemed a lengthy visit.

After Mr Seaga came back downstairs, he and I stood by my garage for about 15 minutes, speaking about many things. He remarked that he hoped I had noticed that he came alone and not with his usual entourage. I thanked him and explained that I was trying to manage this process with as much dignity as I could for Carl. I further explained that I was stretched tightly between handling Carl's care and his persona, and that privacy was an important aspect of the process.

'GIVE STONE OM . . . before it is too late.' To my astonishment and anger, this headline about the Order of Merit and Carl's impending death appeared in the *Gleaner* two days later. It was a quote from Mr Seaga, made at his annual JLP conference. I immediately got him on the phone. I was nearly hysterical, but I tried to sound calm.

'Mr Seaga, I cannot believe that you did this to me.'

'What are you talking about, Mrs Stone?'

'We spoke about dissemination of information and you deceived me and made me feel comfortable by talking about your not taking your entourage with you.'

'But I didn't'

'I am very upset with you. I did not know that you were having a JLP conference. I could not imagine that after we spoke you would go to a public session of the conference and say that Carl is dying. How could you do that? You also know that parliament was discussing the ethics of giving Carl an award at this time.'

'It's a matter of public knowledge and I think that the PNP has deliberately dragged their feet on this.'

'I don't care a s--- about an award, and you know what I am talking about. You could have talked to me privately about this when you were here, and I now know why you wanted to go upstairs to look at Carl.'

'Mrs Stone, to tell you the truth, I don't want to talk about this any more.'

'Well, I want to talk, and you had better listen. I have always been distrustful of politicians and you have made me dislike them even more. Mr Seaga, Carl was right about a lot of things, but he was wrong about you. He thought you could be trusted, he thought you were a good person but he was oh so wrong.'

'Professor Stone does not belong to you, madam, he belongs to Jamaica and that is what I was dealing with.'

'That concept of belonging to Jamaica sounds like damn foolishness.'

'Mrs Stone, you are being irrational.'

'One thing I can tell you Mr Seaga, you will never put your foot across the threshold of my house again.'

It was difficult for me to watch Carl through all the stages of the deterioration of his health. The first day he was home from the hospital he had been able to walk from room to room, in the days that followed he had struggled with restlessness, then insomnia, all the time getting weaker and weaker. The hospital bed had loomed large in his consciousness and he had refused to sleep on it or go near it no matter how much I coaxed and cajoled. But ten days after his return home, Carl was permanently installed in that bed.

After the fiasco with Mr Seaga, the representatives of the PNP asked me if it would be all right for them to present Carl with the Order of Merit. I spoke to Carl and he agreed to it. On Wednesday, February 24, the Governor General, his AD, the prime minister and several members of the government who were friends of Carl or people with whom he had worked with at the university were present when the Governor General stood by Carl's bedside and presented this award. Fortunately for me, this took place early in the morning with only Carl's mother and mine present, who were visiting at the time and therefore took part in the ceremony. Carl seemed to be aware of everyone and everything taking place and in the end even wanted to reply. The Governor General reminded Carl that he had spoken more than enough over the years and this occasion was a way for the country to honour him and to say thank you for all the contributions he had made to Jamaican society.

I had been consulting Carl's doctors regularly, seeking advice and reassurance, and Dr Grace had visited often. She had forewarned us that Carl might go into a coma or have a heart attack. I tried not to imagine either one. By this time my brothers, Mark, Barry and Leslie, had more or less taken up residence in the family room adjoining our bedroom. I had requested that one of them stay each night. Friends joined them in the vigil from time to time. Sometime late Wednesday night to early Thursday morning, Carl's breathing changed dramatically. Tricia told me that she and Ryan and Danielle (Lisa's two children) had noticed Carl's snoring getting louder.

Dr Grace later confirmed that my husband had slipped into a coma.

Nothing real or imagined, nothing I had seen or read prepared my sensibilities for how I would feel when Carl entered the coma. I sat on a couch across from him almost transfixed by what was happening. I remember that a cricket match between the West Indies and India was being broadcast on the television and some of the family were watching it in the family room. Mark and others tried to entice me to join them for even five minutes. I tried to leave the room and Carl, but could not. Norma, who was always by my side, reminded me that I had not had much sleep for nearly ten days now and none at all in the last 72 hours.

As the hours ticked by I hoped that this particular process would come to an end soon. I knew how much Carl disliked the state of inactivity and that he, like me, would prefer the end to come quickly. I talked with him often during his coma both when we were alone and when relatives and close friends visited with him. Together, Norma and Shelly spoke to Carl during this period. Barry and I visited with him. Carl's mother reminded him that his brother Leroy was coming to see him so he should hold on until then.

As I held Carl's hand or caressed his forehead, impressions played over and over in my head. The image of Carl's friend, Louis Lindsay, a university lecturer who had been present when Carl received his award less than 24 hours earlier. Louis was so agonized to see his friend ill that he could not remain in the room and instead went outside and walked around the yard several times. The image of Colin Reid, one of Carl's best poll interviewers at the time, coming down the stairs after he visited Carl. This tall well-built man was trying hard to control his emotions as he left the house, passing everyone and unable to say a word.

And then there was the haunting image of my nine-year-old son Timothy, trying to help his father move around the bedroom, a perplexed look on his face, and Carl saying, *'Thanks, Timmy, thanks, Timmy...'*

During the first 15 hours of Carl's coma I talked to his doctors, friends and family, and to Carl, all the while trying to quiet the internal dialogue that I was having with myself. First I had to accept the fact that I could not do anything else to help my husband; I would just have to watch him die. I had to try to calm all my internal organs so that I would remain physically well. *How are my children dealing with this?* I asked myself over and over again as I tried to console them.

About 20 hours into the coma, as I sat watching Carl, I started to feel my world disappearing into his. I knew I had to do something to stop this. I literally felt that I might cease to exist. I confided my fear to Norma and she immediately told Dr Grace. Thursday evening the doctor informed me that I needed to leave the room that Carl was in and get some sleep. Dr Grace had advised me that I should try not to stay with Carl for long stretches of time. After that, I tried to follow her instructions and stayed downstairs for as much as possible.

I accepted the sleeping tablet she offered me and lay down in one of my children's rooms. Though I was afraid of what might happen when I was asleep, I had no choice because of my state of mind. I also knew that when I woke up it would be Friday and Carl's brother Leroy would be there to help me, especially with his mother. That was a comforting thought as I fell asleep.

I did feel physically better after five hours rest. On Friday, all my friends and family were there doing everything they could to support me. I spoke with Norma and Shelly about the idea of the children leaving the house that evening. We had done this before to give them a break from Carl's illness. I then talked to the children and gave them a choice of staying or going out. Tricia went to the movies with Shelly's children, and Timothy went to a pre-arranged tennis lesson. I spoke to them about the strong possibility of their father not being there when they came back.

My brothers monitored Carl that Friday. Leroy had arrived from Ottawa, Canada earlier that day and there was a highly charged emotional scene with him, Carl and Mother. Leslie was the one who realized that Carl had gone silent.

Dr Grace was called. Carl was pronounced dead on Friday evening at 5:00 p.m., after being in a coma for about 40 hours.

Within two minutes of my calling the funeral home, a media house phoned to confirm that Carl had died. I pleaded with them to hold off on the story because my children were not at home and were unaware that their father had died. All I could think about was Tricia and Timothy. I did not want them to hear over the radio that their father had died before I had a chance to speak with them. My friend Carol N, Timothy's prep school teacher, volunteered to pick him up from tennis. Dr Winty was there to see me through Carl's body being taken from the house. I thought at least I would spare the children the trauma of that ordeal.

By then the house and yard were filling up with more friends, family and well-wishers. I was trying to prepare myself while waiting for Timothy and Tricia to get home. I started to walk around the yard from back to front to calm myself. As I paced I drank glasses and glasses of water trying to quiet my internal quivering.

Almost everyone realized that I was distressed. Most people hugged me, others whispered their sorrow of Carl's passing. They all had tears in their eyes. As I was pacing, Miss Queenie, a friend of Carl's mother, addressed me,

'Mrs Stone, why are you not speaking to me?' I walked by her without responding. Over the past couple of years she talked to Carl on the phone about politics and world events. A few minutes later, I walked past her again and she asked me a similar question. I decided to go into the living room to speak to Mother about helping me with her friend. Bending over the back of the sofa where Mother was sitting, I tried to talk to her. Mother slipped down into the sofa as far as she could and just nodded to me. She made it very clear that she had overheard the conversation and did not want Queenie to see her. I walked back outside to the porch just in time to hear Queenie telling some others there how good a friend she was to my family and that I was ignoring her.

'Queenie, I don't think you fully understand what is happening here now. Carl has just died. Tricia and Timothy are not here and I am trying my very best to prepare myself to speak to them when they come.'

'I know that Carl just died but that does not give you a reason to ignore me.'

I repeated what I had said.

'I heard you the first time, but I am a close family friend and I should not be ignored in this way.'

In my pacing I passed Queenie several times and each time she stepped in front of me to get my attention, becoming more and more agitated.

'Queenie, I am sorry but if you feel this way, probably you should leave and come back at a time when more attention can be paid to you.'

'I will not be ignored. I am a close member of this family circle and I should be here at this time.'

As I looked around desperately for help, Leroy came to my rescue. He spoke to Queenie calmly and quietly. She said she would leave but it took Leroy at least an hour to inch her toward the gate.

While this was taking place Timothy arrived. Carol had told him that his father had died. He immediately ran up the stairs to our bedroom and his cries of agony and grief reverberated through the house. Timothy ran from our room to his bedroom, howling. I was grateful to Carol, John and later Leroy for their help in dealing with Timothy. Within half an hour it was time for me to go and pick up Tricia at the movie theatre at Sovereign Centre, five minutes away from home. Timothy insisted on accompanying me. As I picked up Tricia it was Timothy who told her.

'Tricia, Daddy is dead. Tricia, Daddy died, Daddy died.'

'No, no. My Daddy is not dead. No, no.'

Tricia screamed and screamed. She stopped only when Timothy turned on the radio. The airwaves were filled with tributes to Carl. She tried to change the station but the report on his death and the tributes were everywhere.

I stopped the car on Paddington Terrace so that we could all cry together, and so that I could compose myself before returning to the house.

My friends and family tried to provide comfort and consolation. Tricia was upset that I had removed Carl's body before she came home. Timothy was more concerned about what we were going to do with his father's body. He had overheard Leroy and me talking about cremation and announced that no one was going to burn his father. Leroy again came to my rescue and explained the process to him.

Later that evening after receiving dozens of calls from all over the world, I was reminded that I needed to send out a news release to the various media houses. The wife of the former prime minister, Mrs Beverly Manley, with her background in journalism, had advised me to write a news release. She said that she would ensure that everyone who printed or aired any kind information for public consumption would get a copy as soon as possible. She assured me that it was better for the media to have an authorized family news release than to be seeking the information elsewhere. I would always be grateful for her advice.

I was relieved to relinquish most of the planning of the Thanksgiving Service to Dr Winty and Norma. I made only two requests on behalf of Carl. Recordings by Bob Marley and a performance by the University Singers had to be a part of the service. I asked Monty Blake of Meritones fame to do the Bob Marley request and he recorded a whole suite of Carl's favourite Marley songs, along with a song by Third World that played during the musical prelude from 1:45 p.m. to 2:20 p.m., just before the formal service begun.

Days and nights seemed to merge between the day

of Carl's death and his thanksgiving service five days later. I do not remember sleeping, but I must have slept. I do not remember eating but I must have taken in a few bites of food. I must have done all the normal personal preparations for Tricia, Timothy and myself that were required for such an occasion. I know that my friends helped me tremendously. Though I was surrounded by scores of friends and family who gave me love and support, I experienced feelings of isolation and inadequacy that were tied up with the loss of Carl and the secret of HIV/AIDS.

Dr Winty's planning skills were evident at the service, from the erection of the tent outside the University Chapel to the programme itself. As I entered the chapel that evening I was comforted to see familiar faces. I steeled myself for what I knew was to come: the television cameras for the live broadcast, photographers from the other media houses, politicians, members of the diplomatic core who were mostly strangers to me and scores of Jamaicans from all walks of life, some of whom applauded each time a politician entered the chapel.

I worried for Mother. Dr Matt helped to alleviate my concerns by sitting close by and monitoring her. And though I had tried to prepare my children for the service as best as I could, I also worried how they would get through all of this. After the Kingston College Choir's item in the musical prelude, Timothy asked me if the service was over and if he could go home now. With a wry smile I explained to him that he would have to wait until Daddy's colleagues, the people Daddy worked with, marched in and took their places and then the service would begin. As it progressed, I took his programme and periodically pointed out to him where we had reached in the order of service: the University Singers performance, Prime Minister P.J. Patterson and the Leader of the Opposition, Edward Seaga, as they read lessons.

While listening to 'Reflections' by Dr Winty, I paid close attention to the words being spoken.

REFLECTIONS ON A DEPARTED FRIEND –
Eulogy

Excerpts

The basis of a friendship, filled with respect, was laid when I became painfully aware that his mind was as sharp as a surgeon's scalpel cutting through the redundant tissue to reveal the essence of the problem at hand . . .

He was seen wherever the people were found; in their places of work, their organizations, [formal or informal], their institutions, their recreation centres, on the corner with the youth, on the beach with fishermen, with higglers, snow cone vendors; anyone . . .

In the final twenty months of his life his work in communities intensified at an extremely rapid rate. He is recorded on realms of video footage. He produced two national surveys, ten community surveys in ten parishes, one regional survey for the inner city of Kingston, a total of thirteen surveys all delivered on time notwithstanding his university professorial responsibilities in teaching, research and publishing. He prepared a wide variety of background papers which he presented night and day in numerous workshops and seminars, lasting sometimes as long as five days . . .

I wanted to be attentive because I hoped that somehow his words would help to ease some of the dread I felt inside. On behalf of Carl, I found myself listening to the remembrance by Dr Edwin Jones, a friend and colleague of my husband.

REMEMBRANCE – *Carl Stone OM, CD*

Excerpts

Direct and sustained contact with ordinary Jamaicans was a constant factor that energized Carl and his work. Thus he completely revised traditional forms of detachment that had once separated the university from the ordinary people. For his contribution to this process, as well as for his principled defence of the under class, he has been appropriately lionized as a 'roots man' . . .

Beyond that required for sustenance of basic needs and security of family, Carl Stone held disdain for material objects and symbols. We called him 'Cephas' mainly because he set himself as a 'rock-stone' against materialism. Neither power nor money, nor high honour could seduce him ...

Authentic, practical Jamaican man he was, Professor Stone loved a good fete and he loved fellowship. This 'roots man' knew, embellished, and freely used a wide range of Jamaican four-letter words . . . for dramatic effect. He intellectualized about reggae as well as he danced to it. None could outdo his raucous laughter. And he always told a good story. No discerning eye was necessary to see that Carl kept the most disorganized office in the Faculty of Social Sciences. Nor was any needed to see that he was cerebrally the faculty's most organized member.

As he concluded I concurred with all the sentiments and the accolades. As thoughts of Carl's accomplished life swirled around in my head, I wondered if there was any way to come to terms with HIV/AIDS. On an occasion like this when cameras are all around and in your face, when in fact everyone is looking at you, can the mind maintain a sufficient balance to allow the body to move and behave in an appropriate manner? This, at the bare minimum, I wanted to accomplish, and I knew that Tricia's and Timothy's hands in mine would help to give me strength.

As the collection was taken to begin the Carl Stone Scholarship Fund, I hoped I would be around long enough to help expand the fund. I hoped I would live at least a couple of years longer than Carl did with the disease, but more immediately, I hoped I would be able to make it through this day and get home without breaking down.

When it was our time to join the recessional, I gripped Tricia and Timothy's hands. As we left the chapel, I urged Norma to get the car that would take us take home. Articles on HIV all recommend the avoidance of stress; in fact most of the research on major illnesses regard stress as negative. The death of a partner ranks very high on the list of stress-related events. I knew that Carl's dying and all the related consequences, including becoming a single mother and being responsible for raising two children would have a negative impact on my health and the length of my life.

As I stood on the grounds of the chapel waiting, I felt what could be the beginnings of hysteria. My insides began to thaw as if they had been frozen. I felt like crying, but the tears were not coming from my eyes. They were coming from deep inside my abdomen, travelling upwards to choke me. But I would not allow that to happen in front of hundreds of people. Still, I was not sure that I would be able to stop the crying and I did not know how my body would respond to all of this. I kept looking around for Norma and the car. Photographers snapped pictures of the family with politicians. Finally I saw Norma driving up in the car and as I went towards it, one lady in the crowd remarked, 'but dis ya fambily nah grieve, how nobady na cry?'

It was the beginning of summer, nearly three months since Carl's funeral. An ebb and flow of panic and rationality seemed to have taken over my thoughts and become a part of my daily life. There were the days when the panic was overwhelming, when I felt that death was near and I was going to be taken from my children. Yet, the rational part of my brain kept telling me that nobody just gets up and dies, even with HIV. I would probably have to get sick first.

When anxiety threatened to invade my thoughts, I pushed it aside, thinking of all the things that I had to impart and share with my children while I still could.

One of the stories I wanted to share with them was that of my memorable internship at Baxter's Mountain. I thought about it for a few weeks and then decided to take them, along with my sister, Andrea, on an impromptu trip. As we journeyed through the winding roads of upper St. Andrew into St. Mary, I tried to describe Baxter's Mountain to them, trying to help them to see it through my eyes. Even though Baxter's Mountain, for me, had held many challenges, it represented a tranquil space in my life, a place I wanted my children to be aware of, to hold in their memory for later life. As we reached the coastal town of Annotto Bay and turned up into the hills, memories flooded my being. I told Tricia and Timothy about the river and how important a part the river had played in our existence at Baxter's Mountain. Back then, as soon as it started to rain in the hills we knew that school had to be dismissed, so children could get home before the river 'came down'. In those days, we had to take off our shoes to cross the river. When Andrea and the children and I reached Fort George, I realized that modernization had come to Baxter's Mountain in the form of a bridge.

We arrived at the school at Baxter's Mountain and got out of the car to walk around. As we walked, I spoke to Tricia and Timothy about some of my memories of a time so long ago – yet still so precious to me. We walked up to the house of Mr and Mrs Henderson, who had been the school's caretaker and cook for many years. When Mrs Henderson hugged me, I felt the warmth that I had come to associate with her and her husband. While Andrea and I chatted with Mrs Henderson, she brought me up to date on her children. Other members of her family took Tricia and Timothy to explore the woody farmland.

GOOD FREN' BETTA DAN PACKET MONEY

Good friends are invaluable

THERE ARE MANY REASONS why I did not share my HIV-positive status with friends and family. I knew on January 25, 1992 that ours was no ordinary crisis, but at the time I did not have the physical strength or the mental courage for revelations. I decided to go by instinct in terms of disclosure. Whether I told someone was based not only on whether that friend would be loyal but also whether he or she could endure hearing such horrific news. I also had to ascertain how much of a role I would have to play in their grief.

In early February when I found out that I too had been infected with HIV, one of the issues that Carl and I discussed was whom we would tell. My friends had all known – indeed all of Jamaica had known – that Carl was ill. The public diagnosis went from diabetes to no diabetes. Afterwards it was some kind of cancer, then myeloma. The final diagnosis, AIDS, was known only by Carl's three doctors and me.

My closest girlfriend of 20 years, Lisa, and her husband Phillip went through all the pre-AIDS concerns with Carl and me, but as friends we became unglued during this period. Lisa and I disagreed on almost everything. When Dr Errol told us that Carl might have myeloma, I wanted to talk to him alone to get a sense of what I was up against. Lisa vehemently objected on the grounds that I was hurting myself unnecessarily. She drove me to the doctor, but her displeasure was evident. After leaving the doctor's office I was distraught and overcome with grief. She kept telling me that I had made the wrong decision. I had known I needed to get the information. Over the next couple of weeks we hardly had a meeting of the minds, and coupled with the fact my other girlfriends seemed to be on the same wavelength with me, Lisa pulled away from me both emotionally and physically.

Carl and I decided not to tell anyone right away. We thought we needed time to digest and assimilate the information ourselves. We had already established that in all decisions, while we would both talk about them democratically, I would have the final say. Early on, Carl brought up the question of whether to tell Lisa and Phillip. He knew of my deep attachment to them. I told him that my instinct suggested we should not say anything just yet, and after a short discussion with Carl saying, 'are you sure Rose, are you sure', we decided that for the time being I would not.

There were a few times during 1992, when Carl was ill, that I ached to tell Lisa but we were never in sync mentally and emotionally. Certainly all the bonds that we seemed to have shared mentally were no longer evident. Carl had taped an interview (which turned out to be his last) with Ian Boyne on the programme *Profile* that would be aired in November. I was nervous because he was so ill; I had my doubts as to whether he could get through it. I was also very distressed over how Carl might look on television. I had a strong gut feeling that I wanted to share with Lisa what I was going through, so I called her and told her about the taping. She was civil but unimpressed with the whole idea of Carl being on television because, she said, he had done it so many times before. On Sunday I called her and reminded her about the programme and the 5:00 p.m. airing. I called her again after seeing the broadcast with lots of questions on my mind and a willingness to entertain disclosing to her that Carl and I were HIV positive. When she answered the phone, I asked if she had watched the interview, and she answered no. She said she had to cook and look after her children and had not remembered it. I felt rebuffed. I knew I would never again have the feeling that I could confide in her. The opportunity to share with Lisa was lost.

With Norma, I had not shared the many years of friendship that I had with Lisa but in the period 1990 to 1992 we found many common interests. We were seeing the same movies, reading the same books, sharing our views on Jamaica and the social and political process and most important, we were talking and arguing about men and their relationship with each other and their women: their wives, their mothers, their mistresses and their girlfriends.

Most of these discussions emanated from the books we were reading. One of the books we read, *And the Band Played On: Politics, People and the AIDS Epidemic,* by Randy Shilts, chronicled the search for a retrovirus that was responsible for the outbreak of AIDS in the homosexual community in California and New York. A segment of the book explored the disagreement between French research doctors and the British and

American research doctors over who was to be given credit for the discovery of the virus. Norma and I were both moved by the contents of the book and we had many discussions about the implications of what we read.

In our quest to find out what was ailing Carl, my husband and I visited Dr Charles an ENT Specialist who advised us 'to do the AIDS test and get it out of the way'. That same evening I spoke to Norma by phone about the strong suspicion I had that Dr Charles had made an informal clinical diagnosis but he had not revealed it to me. I recall telling her on the phone that what I had to say to her was very private and personal. I told her she was not allowed to ask me any questions right now and that she was not to bring up the subject again until I did, and if I never did we were never to speak about this again. She agreed, so I began.

'Norma do you remember that book that we read where the doctors were quarrelling over who was responsible for finding the virus?'

'Yes. Very well.'

'I think that is what Carl has.'

'No, No, No…'

'The doctors have not told me anything yet but I am 100 per cent sure that Carl has that virus.'

'How can you be so sure?'

'Remember, no questions. What I am asking you to do is to go along with me, with what I have to do to deal with this.' I heard Norma crying. 'Norma, this is not the time to cry because you have to help me.'

'I am not crying, it's just my sinuses.'

'Forget what I have just told you for the time being.'

A few days later when Dr Grace confirmed the diagnosis and also supplied our cover-up diagnosis, cancer of the lymphatic system, I made two phone calls, one to Norma and one to my sister Andrea. When I spoke to Norma there was no hint of our previous conversation; she just did as I had asked her to do – tell my friends that Carl had lymphatic cancer. A week later my family was visiting me. Carl was not at home. By this time I had been tested for HIV but my diagnosis had not yet been made. I was distraught. My friend John called to find out how Carl was doing. I was sobbing so loudly, I was inconsolable. John, unable to speak to me, called Norma to find out what was happening because it seemed to him that I was too distraught and a little bit out of control, he wanted to see me up at Norma's.

That evening at Norma, John said. 'Rosie, I know you love your husband very much, but if you continue to be so out of control you will hurt yourself and you have to be around to nurse him back to good health. Cancer is so common now and there are many good stories about recovery. The medical profession has gone a far way in the treatment of cancer and I believe that Carl will be okay. There are so many different kinds of treatment that they have for cancer so all we have to do is some research and find out the best place in the world to go for treatment.'

As I listened I contemplated whether I should tell him. John continued, 'Norma, tell her, tell her that everything will be OK.'

I looked at Norma. Her face held no indication that she knew the truth. She was definitely prepared to go along with anything I wanted to do.

'I am trying to John, I am trying to,' she said.

'Many cancers are curable,' said John 'and while I should not make comparisons with illnesses, at least there is hope with cancer – it could be worse, it could be AIDS. They have not even developed any proper drugs yet.'

A sob escaped me. John stopped and looked at me and then at Norma. I glanced at Norma and her face was still stoic. John turned to me. I said, 'It is AIDS John. Carl has the virus that leads to AIDS.'

John's mouth was agape, and he was finally silent, but just for a while. 'We can fight that too,' he said.

Norma had tears running down her cheeks. That experience for me was traumatic as I talked to them about the sequence of events leading up to that point. The toll that that first disclosure to two of my most trusted friends took on me was so severe, I wondered if I could ever share this information with anybody else. I felt as if my heart was being torn apart. What further added to my distress was that Lisa came looking for me because Carl had called her and asked if she knew where I was. You could feel the tension in the air when Lisa arrived. A week later I had to say those gut wrenching words to Norma and John: 'I am HIV positive too.'

Early in 1992 I got the strong sense that I wanted to share my HIV status with Dr Matt. I was visiting with Norma at her ballet studios and got up suddenly to leave. I told her what I was going to do, and she wanted to discuss the matter. But I smiled and left for the University Hospital, thinking that for me, even with such an understanding friend as Norma, some decisions are not up for discussion. Luckily for me, Dr Matt was still at the hospital and I asked him if I could see him later. This began as a sharing of information with someone I trusted with my life and the life of my children. He had more knowledge than I did about major illnesses and their impact on families. He also had the expertise and finesse to effectively pass on some of this to me. With him I found a safe place to cry and to say exactly what was on my mind without fear of judgement.

He would sit across from me behind his desk, listen to my ramblings of distress and identify what I needed to pay attention to at that moment. A simple but helpful hint to me was to pay attention when I was driving. When I became lost in thought I would remember his advice and immediately concentrate on the road so as not to compound an already bad situation by having an accident. The 'crying room', as I called Dr Matt's office, became one of my havens during the year that Carl was ill and until shortly after he died.

Dr Barry also gave me invaluable support during 1992–1993, the year that Carl was ill, by allowing me to call his house, even at midnight, if Carl was feeling low. He would listen as I told him how Carl was feeling that day, the symptoms, his temperature and his weight, all of which I had written down. It was reassuring to me to have a doctor supporting me in this way because it made me feel that I was doing the right thing for Carl. I became so obsessed by Carl's fluctuating weight and temperature, however, that Dr Barry eventually advised me to throw away both the thermometer and scale.

In the summer of 1993, about six months after Carl died, I told three people about my HIV status. I had just returned from my seven-day, three-city tour of Europe and was in a Home Depot in Florida with my sister Rena, her children and mine. While waiting in line with Rena I felt I was going to have one of my fainting episodes. I asked Rena to help me to find a bathroom and I went into an enclosure and held on until I came out of the faint. When I came back to join my family, Rena asked if I was all right. I told her that I was just a little light-headed, that my ears were popping and that it was probably the long flights that I had taken recently.

How to deal with my dread was quite another matter. I was quite well during my trip. I wondered if travel had put too much stress on my system, and was hoping that this was not the beginning of the end, as far as my undisclosed disease was concerned. I allowed myself a few minutes of panic and by the time we were back at Rena's home, I had a strong need to tell Leroy, Carl's only sibling. The Stone family had been giving me such a hard time that I resolved to inform the one who was the least threatening to me: that was Leroy. I would have to call him from Rena's and be very careful.

'Leroy, I have something very important to tell you.'

'Go ahead Rose, go ahead.'

'I am ill too, like Carl was and I thought that one member of Carl's family should know.'

'I am so sorry to hear that Rose, is this a recent diagnosis? I hope it was not brought on by the stress of dealing with Carl.'

'I was diagnosed a few days after Carl. Leroy I am trying

to tell you something so you have to read between the lines. The story of Carl's illness is just a made up one to protect Carl and myself in particular and the family in general.'

'I do not understand. The family is not in need of protection from two of its members getting cancer.'

'I contracted the disease from Carl. It is an illness that you can get from your partner. A wife can give it to her husband and vice versa.'

'I am totally confused.'

'Leroy I am trying to tell you something that is very difficult for me to say. There are children moving about, coming in and out of the area that I am in, I am pretending to have a normal conversation with you, so think of all that I have said.'

'Rose, I have to call you later.'

'Oh, I know something that will help you to understand. Arthur Ashe contracted the same thing.'

There was a long pause as Leroy tried to digest this information.

'I wish I did not have to tell you, but I panicked earlier today. I hope you can keep it to yourself because I have not told one member of my family yet.'

'You can depend on me for at least that Rose, discretion. I feel so much worse about how my family has behaved towards you and I am certainly going to put on my thinking hat to see in what ways I can help you.'

'This call is for information only, no help required.'

'I would like to help Tricia and Timothy, I think some input from me could help you even as far as planning is concerned.'

'We will see what happens in the future. The truth is, I would like to stay away from your family.'

'How are you feeling? You have gone through so much. I will call you soon. This is such distressing news. There is an upside: Arthur Ashe seems to be doing well.'

'No Leroy, Arthur Ashe is dead. He died a few weeks before Carl.'

Several times during 1992 and 1993 I felt like disclosing my HIV status to Shelly. At the time, however, it seemed so complicated. Telling her would involve revealing my health status to an entire family. Tricia and Timothy were interacting daily with Shelly's three girls. Shelly, in particular, and a few other friends were helping me by doing a lot of the activities with my children that I wasn't capable of doing during the year that Carl was ill until his death and the beginning of the grief process.

One day Shelly and I were alone on a trip to Ocho Rios to do some business related to a cottage that Shelly and her husband, Peter, owned at the time. Shelly, a teacher, stopped teaching for some time to stay at home to raise her children. I had the opportunity to tell her the truth, but I was so busy concealing the fact that I was ill that day from the AZT medication that I could hardly think straight. I pretended to have developed a bad case of carsickness so that I would have an excuse to eat dry crackers and suck on a lot of mints, in order to keep myself from being sick. The day was torturous for me. To find a couple of hours of respite on a lovely day with a close friend was unusual, and otherwise would have been welcome but I was so sick and confused that all I could do was to try to survive it.

I was in Florida that summer of 1993, a few months after Carl died. Peter and Shelly were there as well. Shelly and I spoke on the telephone a few times and she, probably sensing my distress, invited me to lunch. I mentally prepared myself for the ordeal of revealing my health status to a close friend to whom I should have had the courage to tell the truth much earlier. My friendship with Shelly had been easier and less complicated than my relationship with some other girlfriends. I was depending on Shelly's easy and relaxed style to help us through. During lunch I told her everything about the HIV, the cover up, the lies and the deception. I tried to give her a flavour of what I had gone through those last 18 months. I explained the scare I had had earlier on in Florida and said that I did not think I could travel again. I also said that I did not know how long I had to live. Shelly did not interrupt as I painted a worst-case scenario. Her response was classic Shelly, and I had to smile in the middle of my tears.

'Rose, if you had told me that you had grown a penis I would not be more surprised than I am right now. I am so sorry that you had to go through all of this.'

As we left the restaurant, Shelly asked me if I would tell Peter soon and I said that I would tell him later that day. When I shared the information with Peter, we hugged and cried together as he promised to support me in any way that he could.

December 1991 represented a major shift to the rhythm of my life and that of my family. There seemed no way of predicting with any degree of accuracy how the next minute of my life would play out. Further, I had absolutely no control over the number of steps I would have to make as I tried to hop, skip and jump over the volume and consequences of Carl's indiscretion.

The one aspect of my life that I could try to manage was when and to whom I would disclose my HIV status. This was very hard for me to do in Jamaica. Rumours were everywhere. Some good friends, some acquaintances and even people I hardly knew asked me directly if Carl had AIDS. Others hinted at it and I had to lie to all of them. The conversation at least ended when I denied it.

I turned to Dr Grace to help me. I hoped that by talking with her it would help me to quiet my trepidation. As we spoke, the question of moral responsibility seemed to be central to my dilemma. Did I have a moral responsibility to my friend Lana, my dentist and Carl's, to disclose my HIV status? What about her as a professional – was it not up to her to use safety precautions in dealing with all her patients? Were these questions I should be worried about? Or were they irrelevant to my ongoing crisis? Could ideals of friendship be suspended in time while I just went into pragmatic survival mode? Was I wasting valuable mental energy on an issue that should not concern me?

As we discussed these issues, I felt the unease with my behaviour slowly leave me. Dr Grace expressed the belief that all medical professionals should be protecting themselves and that she was sure that my friend would do an AIDS test soon. She also believed that I had enough to deal with right now and that sometime in the future I could revisit the friendship issue. I felt better, but it did not prevent me from worrying and calling Lana to find out discreetly how she was. Over time she told me she had had the AIDS test and it was negative, and my relief was beyond measure.

The concern that had paralyzed me and prevented me from telling Shelly earlier was multiplied one hundred fold at the thought of disclosing my illness to my sister, Shirley. I felt that if and when I told her, I would be telling at least 14 persons. Disclosure to Shirley meant disclosure to a whole village and that terrified me.

And so during the early years, 1991–1995, there were three friends Norma, John and Shelly, and three doctors, Dr Grace, Dr Matt and Dr Barry who provided vital support to me. Aside from a couple of other doctors, these latter three were the only ones who had information regarding Carl and my HIV status. They helped me from crisis to crisis. They are the ones who cajoled, guided and provided practical solutions to my immediate problems.

There were others too whose support was vital because of the unique relationship either Carl or I had with them. One was Dr Winty, Carl's closest friend at the time he became sick. I called on him many times when I was unable to cope, and he visited on other occasions as if he had a radar that told him we needed him. He understood Carl and knew what it took to get him excited and interested at times when my husband felt like giving up. Much later, after Carl died and I asked Dr Winty if he had heard the rumours, he said he had but that as a medical professional he had no time to listen to gossip. When friends and others had tried to spread the rumours, he had had to shout at some, have words with others or simply hang up the phone. It was while we were having this conversation that I told him what had really happened to Carl and me. He listened intently and told me that he had a great deal of respect and admiration for how I handled the whole matter. He also said that he would not have done less for Carl, with or without knowing what I had shared with him.

The other person I could not have done without was Andrea, my youngest sister. After Carl died, Andrea moved in with Tricia, Timothy and me to become a part of our immediate family. She was going to help me, as she always did, in ways that only she could, to buttress the children and me. Many times the thought of telling her about my illness crossed my mind. In the end, however, my knowledge about her personality prevented me from doing so. I knew that when I told her, I would truly be telling her alone; she would not share this information with anyone, not friends or family members. I thought that she needed to know in conjunction with my other sister, Rena, so that they could be prepared when the time came to deal with all the ramifications of my illness. I did, however, ask her on three separate occasions between 1993 and 1995, hypothetically, whether if a friend had bad news to tell her, she would prefer to hear it now or later. She always answered that if it would make no difference to the friend or to the bad news, she would prefer to hear it later.

In March 1993, about a month after Carl died, I took the children to a hotel in Ocho Rios for a weekend. Tricia and Timothy's friends were going to be there too, and I hoped that my children would get some comfort from their presence. While there I began to think of the enormity of telling my children, my parents and my seven siblings that Carl had died from complications associated with AIDS and that I had contracted the virus too. I took the hotel stationary and started to write letters. At the time I did not think I could verbalize my thoughts, but perhaps I could get them down on paper. My thinking at the time, amid the grief, was that if I was lucky I could live a year or two longer than Carl had after diagnosis. I was hoping that I would be able to at least give them to Norma so that she could distribute them for me. Tricia and Timothy had already had so much loss in their life that I was unable to envision a time when I would be strong enough to tell them the truth. My letter to them was what I thought was age appropriate and made no mention of my HIV status or Carl's true diagnosis.

March 1993

For Tricia and Timothy

Today is Thursday; I do not know the date. A month or so has passed since your father has died. Lack of courage on my part and some selfishness lead me to think or wish that I had died when he did. But the love that I have for you both causes me to abandon those thoughts and live because of you both and also live because I love life.

I want to say something about your father. He was a very special man, having been given a special gift – that of a great mind. He used it very well and achieved a lot nationally and internationally.

Tricia and Timothy, he was a man and as such had flaws in his personality as do all of us human beings. One thing you have to remember is that he loved all three of us very much. He loved me in a special way because I was his wife and understood him more than anyone else. I also forgave him for any wrong doing that he did to me during the course of his life. I forgave him because I know that it was not wilfully done. But in his humanity he erred many times.

The real reason for his life was Tricia and Timothy. It was for you two that he lived and worked. While he enjoyed his work, you two provided the rationale, the 'why' for his existence. I tell you this not only because it is true but because you must believe it. He loved you both so much. You have to be able to use this love to your advantage.

One way of doing this, if there arises any situation where it demands that you forgive Daddy and me for anything we have done, is to dig deep inside and forgive us. When you find that you cannot, try to forget or just disregard the information as utter rubbish or the stuff of overactive imaginations.

Daddy's first thought when he heard he was ill was 'You mean I am not going to see my son and daughter grow up?' He tried to remain alive for as long as possible just for us. But as you know he lived only one year after we knew he was ill. Daddy did a lot of unselfish things for us and in the last year of his life instead of writing a book or doing something else that would add to his accomplishments he worked to make money so that we would be comfortable when he left us.

I am going to try to do my best by bringing you both up as accomplished and independent adults. Use your knowledge and love for us as pivots around which your lives will blossom.

As I write this letter I am in a lot of pain because I loved your father very much and I miss him more than anyone can imagine. I am going on in life because I love you both. If I could, I would bring back Daddy just for you two.

Life can be tough for some people and I hope that the time that the three of us can spend together will be fulfilling and help us get over the loss of Daddy.

If anything should happen to me (and I hope it won't happen until I am very old), and I am taken away from you through illness or accident be brave and remember that I loved you both very much. Remember that all my family and friends love you too.

Anger and bitterness are emotions that might cross your horizon but do not let them consume you or overcome you. Forgiveness and love are emotions that can lift you up when you are down and help you to go through life with fewer scars than the negative emotions.

You both will have enough financial resources for your needs; use them wisely. They are a gift from Daddy for all his hard work and labour that he so tirelessly undertook. His legacy of hard work, strength of character and his incorruptible nature will help you to be strong. My legacy is loving you all, Daddy, Tricia and Timothy.

Stand firm in my love,
Mummy

MOUT-A-MASSY...KIBBA YUH MOUT!

Chatterbox...Shut up!

IN JUNE 1994 my daughter Tricia had just turned fifteen. She was having the usual acne problems and Dr Andrea, a dermatologist, was trying to help us. We had an appointment for a follow-up visit, but Tricia was not thrilled about going to see the doctor because she felt it was unnecessary. I convinced her to go, and we arrived early for her appointment. The common waiting area was crowded, it seemed as if many doctors were working that day. I glanced around the room and saw the various levels of stress and anxiety on people's faces. A wave of hopelessness and distress washed over me. In the dark recesses of my mind I was thinking about my mortality and how much time I had left with my children. I wanted enough time to help them to be at least independent of me. I was not having a good day. It was now 17 months after Carl died. I was feeling his absence acutely, especially as it related to the children. I needed his help in bringing up these two children. But I hoped my face did not show my feelings.

I asked Tricia if she could go into the doctor's office by herself, as this was just a follow up consultation. She agreed, smiled and said, 'I can do this Mummy.' We talked a little about what was likely to happen in the doctor's office, what type of questions the doctor would ask and how Tricia would answer them. Tricia went in on her own and was out in ten minutes. I asked Tricia how it had gone with the dermatologist, but she told me that the doctor wanted to see me.

As I walked into Dr Andrea's office I tried to focus on Tricia and happy thoughts, to appear normal. In fact, I was wondering why the doctor wanted to see me. Was she going to suggest some new treatment for Tricia?

The doctor greeted me and we shook hands and exchanged pleasantries.

'So nice to see you again.' She smiled broadly.

'You wanted to talk to me about Tricia?' I inquired.

'Oh no, Mrs Stone. I wanted to talk to you about how well you are doing.'

'What do you mean?'

'The whole medical community is so proud of you.' She continued to smile.

'What are you talking about?'

'We all know that Professor Stone died from complications related to AIDS and that you are infected, and we are all so proud of the way you have handled the situation.'

I was shocked into speechlessness. Once again I had entered the twilight zone that sometimes threatened me, and this time I was trapped. What 'whole medical community'? Only a few doctors knew this information and they had assured me that my secret was safe with them. Doctor Andrea continued.

'We were so sorry to lose the Professor. He contributed so much to the society.'

'Did you speak to Carl's doctors?' My voice box had started to work again but discordant sounds were rushing out.

'You are doing so well,' she said as if she had not heard me, 'and I wanted you to talk to someone who is in a similar position as you but not doing so well.'

'Did you speak to Carl's doctors?' I repeated.

She heard me this time and now she was no longer smiling.

'No.' she said, for the first time seeming to notice my reaction.

'No, I did not speak to Carl's doctors . . . but it is common knowledge.'

'Common knowledge? *What* is common knowledge? I really don't know what you are talking about.' I was trying to shout but was feeling totally defeated. Tears began to flow freely.

'But Mrs Stone, while I didn't speak to Carl's doctors, there are rumours.'

'And as a medical doctor, a professional, you have called me in here today to tell me some rumours that the "whole medical community" knows about?' I was trying hard to compose myself.

'Oh no the rumours may have come from medical technicians.'

'You felt compelled to call me into your office to talk to me about these rumours? I can't tell you how strange this whole experience is. I just can't believe this is happening.'

'I am sorry to upset you Mrs Stone, but let me explain.'

'I have to leave now. I don't have any clue *what* you are talking about. The one thing I am sure about is that you do not have to explain any further. It is quite clear to me.'

'But Mrs Stone…'

As I turned my back on Dr Andrea I realized that once again I had been placed in a position where I had only a few seconds to compose myself, to get my emotions under control and to suppress the rage that I felt. I tried to adopt a carefree countenance. My daughter was out there in the waiting room full of people.

As I walked out of Dr Andrea's office, immediately Tricia asked, 'What's wrong Mummy?'

I tried to smile and assure her that it had nothing to do with her.

We made our way to the car and I drove slowly and deliberately from Cross Roads. I was not far from home, about 10 to 15 minutes without traffic delays.

I do not recall the small talk or lack thereof as I tried to slow my racing thoughts, remain calm and concentrate on the road. I wanted to reach home as quickly as possible to call the doctors. As we reached the final traffic light my patience was wearing thin. I remarked, 'Not another red light. We could at least get *one* green light today.'

'Mummy, don't you realize that once we get red at one traffic light, we will get red all the way home?'

'That happens sometimes Tricia. That is how life turns out sometimes: a lot of obstacles to overcome.'

When we arrived home, Tricia came to my arms and hugged me tightly. She must have sensed that I needed a hug badly.

That evening, I called Dr Grace and explained what had happened. She told me that no one had contacted her with the request that Dr Andrea alluded to. She consoled and calmed me as she had been doing for the past couple of years. She told me that she just could not imagine how something as unprofessional as this could happen. She agreed with me that I should make a formal complaint to the Medical Association of Jamaica.

I then called Dr Barry, the pathologist from the University Hospital who had worked with Carl and me on the blood tests. He had been a great guide and comfort to me during the year that Carl was ill. He was incensed at Dr Andrea and he told me he would have a talk with her and then call me back. The following day Dr Barry called to say that Dr Andrea was upset. She told him that she had closed her offices after I left and was now in bed totally distraught. She also wanted to send me a bouquet of flowers. By then I was out of the twilight zone that she had dragged me into. I responded with what was left of my strength by using some of Jamaica's choicest words to tell Dr Andrea where she could stuff her flowers.

In early 1994 when Dr Andrea breached her professional ethics and went whimpering into bed, I did not know how to put the pieces together. Obviously she had felt that our private information could be exchanged among medical personnel. And she had taken liberties by sharing my information with at least one patient of hers. The most puzzling aspect of the whole exchange was that either whoever had given her the information had set her up to believe that I had given permission to the 'whole medical community' to share Carl's and my medical record; or she simply misread the informant and believed that the information was 'common knowledge' and as such, hers to do as she wished.

In October 1994, just a year after Carl died, Tricia called me from St. Hugh's with devastating news. Her best friend, Meisha, had died from an asthma attack. I had just seen Meisha a few days earlier and had spoken to her on the phone when she called to remind Tricia to take notes for her, as she had not been feeling well. I was completely undone by Meisha's death. I wished that I was able to bear some of what I thought Tricia must be feeling. I was proud of her when she read a lesson at Meisha's thanksgiving service. Meisha's parents did all they could to comfort Meisha's young friends. At Dovecot Burial Park, I watched as Meisha's father put his arms around these young people by the graveside, and I marvelled at the way he was able to set his grief aside to offer strength and understanding to them.

At Meisha's house later that evening, I came to understand further how the chatter about our family was everywhere and would affect even normal discourse. While talking to a male relative of Meisha's who was from Portland, east Jamaica, he expressed his sorrow at Meisha's passing, but also his belief that ganja tea could have cured Meisha's asthma. Further in the conversation, he asked me my name. I told him.
'You related to the Professor that died a year ago?'
'Yes, I am his widow.'
'Bwoy, mi sorry dat Jamaica lose a man of that calibre, especially since him die so young. All of us in the district stay up all evening to watch the funeral on TV. Bwoy me really sorry him dead.' We were silent for a while

as I thought about what he just said.

'Mrs Stone, I can ask you a personal question?'

'Sure.'

'What your husband die of?'

'He died from lymphatic cancer.' The lie had become almost automatic. He thought for a moment.

'What a way dem spread rumour on you and the Professor eeh! Dem say he died from AIDS. Bwoy I tell yuh, Jamaicans can really spread rumour. An' me hear from good source, Mrs Stone, that is the doctors spread it. I am very glad to meet and to know that you all right Mrs Stone.'

As I sat on the verandah I felt my whole being try to wrestle with the idea of living the rest of my life lying not only to friends and relatives, but also to strangers.

In February 1996, Tricia complained of pains while attending her ballet classes. She was later diagnosed with appendicitis and admitted to the Tony Thwaites Wing of the University Hospital for surgery. My sister, Andrea, and I were in Tricia's room before the surgery, when the doctor asked to speak with me privately. After the usual pleasantries the doctor said to me, 'Mrs Stone, I understand that your late husband, Professor Stone, had AIDS. I wanted to know if there is any reason why I should test your daughter.'

'Doctor, are you seriously asking me for permission to test my daughter who will be 17 years old in a couple of months and was just in a ballet class?'

To the best of my knowledge, in 1996 in Jamaica, no children born with AIDS lived to see their sixteenth birthday.

'Yes Mrs Stone, I think it is a reasonable request to make.'

As I looked at this young doctor, my first thought was to wonder how he had gained unauthorized access to Carl's medical file and how he could be so comfortable repeating the information to me. Second, was this trained, medical professional operating on rumours? Did it all tie in with Dr Andrea somehow? Hysteria and rage entered my mind and body.

I don't realize that I have moved until my fist connects with the doctor. To my surprise, he falls to the floor. Where did this strength come from? As I look down at him I suddenly realize that I have attracted the attention of several members of staff. I have to get out of here. I feel as if this is a good time to become a raving lunatic. I plan my escape route. I move as fast as I can, doing as much destruction as I can to anything in my path. There are arms grabbing at me but I am moving too fast. I wonder if I am quick enough to evade the security guard at the door. I have to get to my car. I avoid the security guard by throwing myself through the glass door. I wonder if I can get away with this by claiming dementia? That's a side effect of HIV isn't it? As the glass shatters, the security guard grabs me. By now a crowd has gathered. As handcuffs are slapped onto my wrist, I try to explain to the security guard that I am not well, I have dementia…. The doctor brings me back to reality.

'Mrs Stone, I am waiting for an answer.'
I looked straight into his eyes and said, 'Just a minute.'
I was preparing myself to say the words that I felt would betray my family. I should not have to resort to telling this doctor confidential information. But I realized that I was powerless.

I took a deep breath and said, 'My daughter is adopted.'

'OK, Mrs Stone.'

As I walked from him, tears cascading down my face, the physical pain was so severe that I thought I would fall to the ground. Once again the medical community was screwing me and I was defenceless.

As soon as I returned home I called my friend Dr Barry, who worked and taught at the hospital. As I started to relate the incident, the tears began to flow again. He told me that he was so sorry that this event took place and that he was going to deal with this young doctor immediately, as he had with Dr Andrea. By the next day, the young doctor no longer treated my daughter.

Chatter also played an important part in the increasing distance between me and my friend Lisa. In April 2000, seven years after Carl's death, in an attempt to reconnect with Lisa, I telephoned her. We had drifted apart when I chose not to tell her in 1992 that Carl and I had contracted AIDS. Now, I began the conversation by telling her that I had finally started to put on paper some of our experiences in relation to AIDS. I reminded her about Father Tony, a priest and counsellor, and how instrumental he had been in encouraging me to write. Father Tony thought a work of this kind would help Jamaicans understand the disease.

I also told her that I had talked to my friend Earl, who taught philosophy at the university and who had written many books. We had spoken mainly about the problems that might arise from publishing a story that was so deeply personal. Earl's fears centred on the cruelty of our society in these matters and he mentioned that the cruelty might be directed, not only at my immediate family, but also at the public's memories of Carl and his accomplishments. Lisa listened and then asked, 'Why are you writing this book anyway?'

I sensed hostility in her tone. 'It is something that I have to do. I feel it deep inside and I think at this time in my life when my ability to contribute to society is severely restricted, this is one way to do so.'

'Are you convinced that you want to write this book as Rosemarie Stone?'

'Lisa, I am very sure about that, but I still have to think about my children, family and even friends. They are the ones that such a revealing book would impact directly.'

'But it seems you are not ready to write such a book.'

'Why do you say that?'

'Well, the way I see it, if you are really ready to write you would not be telephoning anyone to discuss it.'

'You mean I would not be calling *you* specifically.'

'Not just me, but you seem to be talking to a lot of people. If you were really ready you would not need to talk to anyone. Just write your book. It is yours, you shouldn't think about how it affects anyone else except perhaps your children. All you have to do is write it. It is your account. If it hurts anyone, then that is how it is.'

'I don't think you understand that I don't need friends to help me decide if I am to write or not, or whether to write anonymously or not. I have decided to write as truthfully and honestly as I can and I hope that will be enough. But you underestimate the value of dialogue between friends. I wanted to talk to you about how this crisis in my life has damaged our relationship.'

'Rose, let me ask you, would you be writing this book to help people like yourself cope?'

'Oh no. People like me who have access to resources and information find ways to cope. They will find out, like I did, how HIV devours their economic resources. Most infected Jamaicans can't relate to spending US$1,500 per month for medication. Sadly a large percentage of them will go through their HIV lives without access to the life-saving drugs that I have taken. But if what I write helps anyone, it would be a by-product, a bonus. That really is not my intention.'

'You know they are going to crucify Carl.'

'But he has been dead for over seven years.'

'You obviously have not listened to talk radio and heard Wilmot Perkins talk about Carl.'

'Lisa, do you really think that I would allow Wilmot Perkins or any media personality to prevent me from doing something that is so important to me?'

'It is a fact that when people are successful or as well known as Carl was, other people will do their best to pull them down.'

'OK, I know that, but I have already considered some of your concerns over the media. In any case, I think the media has been very good to me and I think that time will minimize any harshness. I prefer to remember Wilmot Perkins as someone who came to see Carl a few times when he was ill. I know Carl enjoyed some Sunday mornings with him and his wife. Also Carl and Wilmot had long discussions on the phone around that time.'

'You know that sometimes when I am around other people and I mention Carl's name or his contribution to society, there is a hush. That tells me that the people around me would prefer me not to speak about him.'

'Really? You are telling me that in your circle of friends the fact that Carl committed adultery and contracted AIDS offends their sensibilities so much that they cannot talk about him or any contribution he might have made? I find that hard to believe.'

'You know they say he was bisexual?'

'Yes. But that's the chatter. And what you mean is homosexual,' I said jokingly. 'But that talk always comes with the AIDS landscape in Jamaica. People assume that if you are a man and you have contracted the virus, you must be homosexual.'

'No, no. He had sex with other women and you. That wouldn't be homosexual.'

I realized that my attempt at humour had been lost on my friend Lisa and she was seriously trying to educate me on the difference between bisexuality and homosexuality.

'Lisa, listen very carefully to my question and answer truthfully. Do you think that Carl was anything other than a heterosexual?'

'No, I personally think he was heterosexual – but they say he was not.'

'Who are "they" really? Your friends?'

'Well, people who I hear it from. The rumours are everywhere.'

'Its one thing to hear rumours but it's quite another thing to repeat them.'

'You should not worry about any of those things anyway

– you will get a lot of sympathy and compassion because you didn't do anything. You are the victim.'

'I would certainly not be writing to get sympathy, and I am not a victim. I had a 20-year relationship with Carl and I believe that I must share some responsibility for the fruits of the marriage even if some of them are rotten and indigestible.'

'Do you know that some people see Carl as a dirty, nasty, w----?'

I was speechless, not only at the callousness of the words but at the harshness of its intent. As my mind tried to absorb the fact that the friend that I loved and who I thought had loved Carl could not find the other million ways to convey this information to me, tears started to flow silently down my face. *Well Rosie, you thought you wanted discussion and dialogue? Instead you got brutal words.* This had certainly become a part of my reality.

'Rose, are you still there?'

'Yes, I am.'

'Are you surprised that people are saying these things? 'Lisa, I believe that those are your words. I don't believe that anyone said anything like that to you. And even if someone did say something and that was your interpretation, I am shocked that you would repeat it to me in that manner. I suppose there is nothing else to say.'

'OK Rosie.'

'Bye Lisa.'

Lisa's hurtful words reminded me of an incident much earlier, with Carl's aunt in Florida. In the summer of 1993 when the children and I visited Rena in Florida, Rena took me to visit Aunt G, Carl's Aunt. Aunt G and I had spoken on the telephone during Carl's illness. I had mentioned to her at the time that Mother, her sister, was causing some concern and I was not sure how to handle the situation. Aunt G advised me that I was to do the best for Carl and to ignore Mother and her histrionics because Mother was a strong woman and would get through it OK. While at her home, Rena, the children and I waited for a while before I realized that something was wrong. I asked her caregiver, whom I knew well, what was taking Aunt G so long to come out to see us.

'Pauline, where is Aunt G? We have been waiting for nearly ten minutes now. Is something wrong? Is she ill?'

'No Rose. She is not ill but she is very upset with you.'

'Upset with me?'

As I turned toward Pauline I could see the door slowly opening and Aunt G emerging from her bedroom her face looking like Hurricane Gilbert. She stopped at the door, looked around the living room, ignored Rena and me and said, 'I would like to see the children alone.' Tricia and Timothy got up, and I gave them a picture of the four of us that I had brought to give to her. As Aunt G and the children disappeared into her room I turned to Pauline.

'What did I do?'

'She blames you for everything, even Carl's death. She even said that you prevented her from talking to Carl when she called.'

'That's impossible Pauline. I spoke to Aunt G recently and we were on good terms. What could have happened?'

As the tears began to flow in earnest, Rena began to get visibly upset. 'Rose, let's leave now. You do not need to go through this now. Why is she blaming you for things that are beyond your control? I don't understand it.'

'Rena and Rose,' Pauline interjected, 'I sat and spoke with her about how irrational her feelings were. I told her that one person couldn't be blamed for all of these things.'

'Rose, I think you should get your children and we should leave. How do you know what she is saying to them, especially when she feels that way about you?'

'No, I don't think she would do anything like that Rena.'

'The only way I can explain it is that she is so upset at losing Carl that she needs to blame someone and the only one she can blame is you.'

As we are discussing all of this, Aunt G came out with the children, her face still looking like dark clouds gathering. I took a quick look at the children and they were smiling, so I felt relief. I quickly walked to the door and down the steps to the gate with the children following, so that they would not see that I was crying. In the car, Rena asked Tricia and Timothy about their conversation with Aunt G. They told us that she had spoken a lot about Carl and how much she loved him.

Later that night, I received a call from Aunt G.

'Hi Rose. You notice that I did not talk with you today, but I am so very upset at the death of Carl. He was not only Flossie's son, you know, he was my son too. When he was young and he used to visit me in Port Antonio, everybody thought he was my son,' she paused. 'Rose are you there?'

'Yes Aunt G.'

'I must tell you that when he was a baby, the only thing I did not do for him was to breastfeed him,' she paused.

'I spoke to your children.'

'Yes Aunt G.'

'I wished them well.'

'Yes Aunt G.'

'I have no reason to come back to Jamaica or to visit because my baby is not there anymore. And I have to be straight with you Rose, I would prefer if you don't come to visit or call me again.'

I was unable to speak.

'Rose, I don't mean any ill for the children you know, I just think that this chapter of my life is finished.'

'OK Aunt G.'

As soon as I hung up the phone I called Leroy in Canada to tell him how I felt about the visit and the phone call. At the time I was sure that Mother was the one who had poisoned Aunt G's mind against me. Aunt G, in her grief, with just a few words, completely obliterated a 20-year relationship and there was nothing I could do about it. As in the case with the doctor who circulated my confidential information, I felt powerless to do much more than just file away disappointment and indignation and hope that time would help to make it seem less significant.

W'EN MAN 'AVE HALF A FOOT, 'IM DANCE NEAR 'IM FAMBILY

When a person is ill, he will maintain close ties with family and friends

IN THE SUMMER OF 1995, I decided to take the first steps in disclosing my HIV-positive status to some members of my family. Father Tony, a Jesuit priest and counsellor, had entered my life. I had not died yet from complications connected to my HIV infection and I certainly was not sitting still and waiting for my demise but thoughts of death were my constant companion.

I knew I should go into some sort of counselling, but I was so afraid and distrustful of medical practitioners that I was paralyzed with fear when I thought about going into an office and telling someone who might not be trustworthy. Someone I trusted had betrayed me. More disturbing was the sense I had that some doctors believed they somehow had a right to information on Carl. It seemed to me then, and even later on reflection, that because Carl had contracted HIV they thought he had committed some evil. An evil so vile that his right to privacy was rescinded. My perception was that there was no sense of outrage that the rumours were everywhere and that a doctor spread them. Strangers knew my T-cell count when I did not even know it myself.

I tried to insulate myself from this. I did not spend much time thinking about it, but I confronted the issue when I could. This I did at my peril because it is hard to be the target of a rumour. I could not do any real investigation; I did not have the time or the expertise. I was also, of course, hiding and trying to cover the truth, so that limited what questions I could ask and of whom. I got information from a good source that a doctor of Chinese background who worked at the Medical Centre had, while attending a gambling session, talked about Carl's diagnosis and prognosis. Without thinking it through, I accused a doctor who had treated Carl that he was the one who had betrayed our trust and so had compromised his principles. Midway through my tirade he made it clear that he had never been in a gambling establishment and I realized that he was not the one. At the time, I naively thought that the only doctors who knew about Carl were those we had spoken to directly or those who had legitimate access to Carl's medical file. I learned later, that the 'entire medical community' was privy to Carl's information. I apologized and left the doctor's office, trying hard to forget all the terrible things I had said to him.

In March 1995 my friend Norma came to visit me at home with what she thought was exciting information for me.

'Rose you should have come with me to the Art exhibition.'

'No thank you, I do not want to be on display too.'

'I will not argue that point with you now, but I met the most marvellous man at the show and you are just going to love him.'

'Really now.'

'Let me explain. Remember the counsellor that you

have been looking for, I have found him. He is just right for you.'

'Tell me about him. Is he Jamaican?'

'No, that is why he is such a good fit; your secret will be safe with him.'

'Secret . . . we have to use another word. Dr Andrea made it very clear that, at the minimum, the "whole medical community knows".'

'Forget Dr Andrea, she is small potatoes. It is the doctor who told her about you and Carl that we should be focusing on. Please let's get back to my guy.'

'He has become your guy now?'

'He is highly intelligent and has a well developed sense of humour. I know that this does not matter to you but he is short and balding.'

'Interesting, tell me more.'

'While on the surface he does not seem to be a cultural fit, he is a family counsellor who has been married and divorced. In fact, he got custody of his three children after the divorce.'

'That is very unusual. I suspect that listening to other people's problems is not all he does.'

'In a way that's all he does. He is a Jesuit priest now working in Jamaica.'

'Is he white?'

'Yes.'

'Oh my God Norma, you have lost your mind. You have got the dementia that I might develop.'

'Rosie you are going to just love him and he will be able to help you. I feel it in my bones.'

'A white priest. He has not one strike, but two. I thought you knew me. I am not crazy about organized religion

and he is white. You have got this one wrong, Norma.'
'I hear you Rosie, but all your misgivings are going to be blown away when you meet him.'
'And that would be when?'
'Tomorrow afternoon, tea at my house, just the three of us. Is that a good time for you?'
'You did not make any commitment on my behalf?'
'No. I told him that I wanted him to meet my best girlfriend who he is going to like very much. He will be travelling from Mandeville to Kingston tomorrow.'
'I hope this trip is not just for me.'
'No, he is visiting me, and has business at the convent.'
'At Immaculate, he works out of there?'
'Yes.'
'Strike number three, location, location, location, my appointments with him will have to be after midnight.'

But at tea I met Rev Anthony P. Palazzolo (Father Tony) and liked him immediately. I learned that Father Tony had been the pastor of two small church communities, Lionel Town and Hayes in Clarendon. His many duties included being Chaplain at St. John Bosco Home For Boys and Rector of Bethany Home and Shrine of our Lady of Dunsinane. His duties mainly in the mid-island of Jamaica meant that at least he was familiar with the culture. The fact that he was a Jesuit priest who had been divorced appealed to me because he would have the ability to empathize with my situation.

Over the next several months, in a room at the convent, I spent numerous afternoon sessions with Father Tony trying to make sense of my life. It was difficult for me at first, wounded as I was psychologically and emotionally from having contracted HIV from Carl and having watched him die. I felt guilty missing a man who had completely altered the course of my life by giving me HIV. Father Tony helped me to distinguish between these feelings and the normal grief of a wife for her dead husband. This was a critical first step for me, allowing myself to grieve and miss Carl without guilt.

I struggled with the whole concept of myself as an independent-minded middle-aged woman (I would be 48 in October of that year) finding herself with HIV and how much responsibility I should take for my condition. Father Tony and I spent a long time over this discussing ways that I might have avoided being infected. Should I have left Carl earlier? When? Should I have left at the first hint of infidelity? Father Tony reminded me that a wife need not be a martyr in taking on a husband's misdeeds, and that I should allow Carl, even though he died, to own his infidelity.

During these sessions there were more tears than I care to remember. Each took such an emotional toll on me that I was forced to remain by myself to try to recover. I spoke to him about Tricia and Timothy and how I feared that they were going to be the most affected by what happened to Carl and me. We talked about privacy issues in a small country like Jamaica and how that would affect the children. I talked about the contingency plans I had made in the event that I would not be around.

We worked out a tentative timetable of when to disclose the HIV to family and my children. I came to understand that the longer I waited to disclose to my children, the greater the risk of the 'chatter' reaching them. At the same time I wanted them to be a little older, more mature when I delivered more bad news to them. They had been through so much already in losing their father. Father Tony suggested that one way of gauging the right time to tell my children was to find out where they were in the grieving process. As we were going to be in Florida for a few weeks in the summer he said he would make an appointment with a child psychologist there who would make that determination. He also gave me the name of an excellent child psychologist in Jamaica, Dr Audrey with whom the children would begin some therapy.

It was during one of my counselling sessions that I read to Father Tony the letter that I had written to Tricia and Timothy the week following Carl's memorial service. I had also written letters to other members of my family concerning my HIV infection. He listened with interest and then suggested that some good could come from all of this pain. Father Tony suggested that I write some articles for the Jamaican public that would go some distance toward helping the public to understand those living with HIV and AIDS. I told him I would think about it. He promised that he would arrange everything and protect my identity. I would be doing these articles anonymously. I trusted him.

Five articles were published in the *Gleaner* in October and November 1995.

October 10, 1995

'Protect yourself' by an HIV sufferer

I have been HIV positive for about seven years.

HIV and AIDS are preventable. For those of us already infected there is not much we can do but follow carefully our doctors' directions as we try to keep our bodies and minds as healthy as possible. We have hope that a miracle cure will come along before we depart this earth. . .

But for those who are virus free – do protect yourselves. You cannot begin to understand the multiplicity of emotions that will assail you and the myriad of problems related to family life and friendships when one discovers that one has contracted the AIDS virus.

October 19, 1995

'The pain of discovery' by an HIV sufferer

'The doctor wants me to do an AIDS test!' my partner exclaimed.

'What happens if the test is positive?'

I heard myself say: 'We will stick together and work it out somehow.' My partner repeated the words aloud. These words became the hallmark of both our lives and went a far way in uniting us when pain, guilt and disillusionment made us forget that we had uttered those words of commitment.

October 27, 1995

'HIV sufferer battles for life' by an HIV sufferer

My partner was diagnosed with AIDS, I was HIV positive.

The aftermath of this cleansing was compassion where there was condemnation. I listened to my inner voice that told me that I had the choice to forgive. If peace of mind or something close to it was to be achieved under these circumstances, forgiveness would have to be my choice. As I tried to keep away pain, fear, anger, regret, guilt and sorrow, the strength to forgive became apparent.

November 1995

Gleaner **Article** by an HIV sufferer

As AIDS progresses it pushes against the limits of energy, it is relentless, it is emotionally deleting and eventually it is defeating. (*Clinical Psychology Science Prac.* 1995).

We cannot disclose our HIV/AIDS status just to anyone. There is the fear of social ostracism. There is also the fear of adults using their knowledge of our 'positive' status to stigmatize and discriminate against our children. When I think of my children who have lost one parent being exposed to this kind of added trauma it brings into sharp focus how children have to pay for the misdeeds of adults.

The psychologists' term for our secrets is stressors. They believe that these stressors may be released by disclosure. But the fears of disclosure are real and caution is warranted as when some persons disclose their 'secret' 'their extended family requires that they and their children eat off paper plates when visiting relatives' homes. Additional reports from some mothers reveal that the extended family and friends' physical displays of affection decrease.' (*Clinical Psychology Science Prac.* 1995).

November 1995

***Gleaner* Article** by an HIV sufferer

The celebration of World AIDS Day to someone living with HIV should mean some advancement in the medical research that brings us closer to finding a vaccine or some drug to halt the multiplication of the virus in our bodies. . .

I have learnt personally over these years that it is important to allow others to help us carry the burden of this disease. And I can only say this in retrospect because I did not believe five years ago that I would share this with anyone. I think only people who 'share' the virus can understand the agony, the turbulence and the ambivalence of your very being when you have to share this information with someone else.

While arranging for Timothy and Tricia to go to the psychologist in Florida, I realized that Andrea, my sister who lives with me in Jamaica, Rena, our sister that we would be staying with and her husband Len would all be accompanying us to the office. This could be an opportunity for me to tell these three members of my family at the same time about my HIV infection. I telephoned Norma in Jamaica and asked her to collect the relevant letters and FedEx them to me at Rena's so that they would arrive in time for the appointment. I was also hoping that the doctor's office would be set up in such a way that I could ask the doctor's permission to use one of his rooms for the discussion.

The plan was that I would ask to see the psychologist alone for about ten minutes, then Timothy would come in and I would introduce him to the doctor and say why he was there. After introducing Timothy to the doctor and telling him about Carl's death and that I was worried about his response to it, I was about to leave when I remembered that I had not told the doctor that my children were adopted, and so I did.

I was shocked when Timothy said, 'Oh no, I am not, I have never heard that word in my life. Why didn't you tell me Mom?' I was stunned beyond belief. Carl and I had spoken openly to our children about their adoption as they had to us. Timothy in particular was very vocal in asking questions about his adoption. I spoke to him now and tried to jog his memory about three specific occasions on which he and I discussed it. Timothy continued to insist that he did not know what I was talking about. The doctor then suggested that I should leave and he would start the session. Timothy's look of utter confusion set off alarm bells in my mind.

I got the key for the adjacent soundproof room from the doctor and asked Rena, Andrea and Len to join me there. I told them I had two letters to read to them, one was addressed to Andrea and the other was addressed to Rena and Len. I said I had something that was important but horrific to tell them and they would have to prepare themselves for the contents of the letters. Everybody grew still and silent as we all braced ourselves for what was to come. I read Andrea's letter first.

February 5, 1995

Dearest Andrea,
Of all the letters that I have written, and all those that I might write, this one is the most painful for me.

I am writing this letter because I am ill and have a terminal disease. I do not have any idea as to how this illness is going to translate itself in me and through me.

Three years ago when Carl was diagnosed as having cancer first, then AIDS, my whole world fell apart. But luckily for me, my world was not splintered in tiny pieces as it could have been. Tricia and Timothy were my primary concern and all my actions took them into consideration.

The cover-up of Carl's illness was my idea, because as you can imagine he was in one hell of a position. He had been careless and so endangered his life and mine.

A lot of things will now make sense to you and will explain my behaviour over the last three years. I must tell you that over the last two years I felt dirty and unclean. I tried to stay away from babies (I still do), and a host of other things. You can only imagine how horrible it is to feel that way.

In the beginning, I had a hard time going up to Rena and Len. I wished I didn't have to. Gradually, I began to feel more comfortable at their house.

The year when Carl was sick until he died, represented for me the time in my life when I was most human, unselfish and forgiving. I don't know if I can ever again reach that pinnacle of total selflessness. I thought and lived only for others (Carl, Tricia and Timothy).   E reapesca of whenever

I took medication for one and a half years that made me nauseous, ill and very fat (smile). The taking of the medication was sometimes worse than knowing I had a terminal illness. I don't know if I can explain to anyone how it is that Carl and I remained husband

and wife up to the time that he got seriously ill. It could be that we really loved each other, or that the better alternative was to stay close together and we would get through it better, or probably because it was I who organized the 'cover-up' and that things evolved the way they did.

The cover-up was important to me because it was the only way I could see myself surviving under the circumstances. I hope you understand that I never ever thought for one second that I would tell any member of my family. The pain is too much to bear and you will all have a lifetime after I am gone, so I thought the less you knew the better. I told some other people which might surprise you.

Norma – hinted to her before I was sure, so she knew from the beginning.

John – told both Norma and him two to three days after Dr Grace told me.

Dr Matt – told him a few days after I knew.

Shelly and Peter – told them the summer of 1993.

Leroy – told him the summer of 1993.

As you can imagine, I trusted these people with the information because I could not make it through alone. Their support was invaluable.

If anything should happen to me, I am leaving my children in Rena's and your care. All the people whom I have named will help you in any way they can.

I am going to ask you to keep the silence and cover-up for as long as possible because of Tricia and Timothy. I believe there is going to come a time when even they will be able to handle the truth. I am depending on you to know when that time will be.

I am writing these letters when I can because I know the will to do so will leave me when I least expect it. I love you. Please take of my children.

Rosie

I made sure that I read the letter without taking my eyes off the pages. Tears spilled from my eyes. I got choked up and had to stop several times. I tried not to look at the others as I bent my head and waited for my recovery. I read the following letter that had been written to Rena and Len.

Rena and Len's letter

January 24, 1995

Dear Rena and Len,

As I write this letter to you both, I wish that life had been kinder to me than it has. An important area of my life, parenting, has been truncated by the death of Carl and I am finding it increasingly difficult to love my children and parent them at the same time. You might say that the two are not divisible and under normal circumstances they are not.

I find that over the past five years I have had to cope with the abnormal or to put it another way, deviations from the norm. One might ask the question, what is the norm when it comes to life and living?

And I would answer that somewhere my life took some turns that left me digging deep in all of my stored-up resources of love, courage and forgiveness and using these to help me to carry on with the business of living.

When I can no longer go on living it is to you I am entrusting my children. I am depending on both of you, along with Andrea to carry all of the weight of caring physically for them. My wish is that I could live another five years, but one never knows, hence the contingency plans for them.

There are a lot of details that are not in this letter but please ask Andrea to share her letter with you both.

You can speak to Norma and Shelly; they will help you to fill in the blanks. Norma, in particular, has had the enormous burden of knowing from the beginning.

Both Norma and Shelly have a lot of expertise in many areas and know the direction I would like my children to go in. I hope they will be able to help you if I am not around.

One thing we cannot control is John Public and what people will say, even close relatives. I believe in arming Tricia and Timothy with the ammunition they will need to exist in what could be a cruel and devastating world for them.

The ammunition has to come from the love that Carl had for them. He, even more than I, wanted Tricia and Timothy badly. He needed them for his existence. Even though he had personal goals and dreams, in the end they were all bound up in his hopes for his two children whom he loved so much.

They must also know that Carl and I loved each other very much and even towards the end of his life we were husband and wife. That was how our love and passion for one another enabled us to go through hell and not be consumed by the fires.

They must also know that the economic well-being that they might enjoy was the result of all the hard work done by Carl.

You can fill them in on the part I played in their lives. That memory will be more recent and therefore more retrievable.

I will probably write again, but you can imagine the pain I am in at this time as I try to reconcile the fact that one day I might have to give up my children. Please love them for me.

Rosie

When I was through reading, I glanced up and saw that everybody had tears in their eyes. The atmosphere was thick with the weight of my disclosure. They all hugged me and promised to help me in any way they could.

We left the 'room of revelation' and went into the waiting area, where Tricia and her cousins, Kisha and Kino, were waiting for us. We knew that we had to leave the outward manifestations of my disclosure in that room. Our muddled thoughts and emotions had to be disguised in order to deal with the children as naturally as possible. When Timothy's appointment was over, I went into the psychologist's office to have a final few words. He reported to me that in his opinion the trauma of Carl's death had caused Timothy to forget that he was adopted. The psychologist remarked on how well my family seemed to be handling the new reality that I had just divulged. But I felt that it would have been better if I had died and they had read the letters for themselves. I hated to be the cause of so much pain.

A few months later, I told Tricia and Timothy the truth about why their father died and that I too was ill. Father Tony had been instrumental in giving me the tools and preparing me mentally for the disclosures up to that point. He had then returned to the United States for another assignment. I knew that I needed a few counselling sessions before I could disclose to my parents and my three brothers, Mark, Barry and Leslie, so I spoke to Father Howard, an Anglican priest. On the day of the planned disclosure, my brother, Mark, could not be found. His absence suggested that he was not prepared to deal with my disclosure at that time. I, along with Father Howard, decided that I should just read to everybody the letter that I had written to my parents, and leave right afterwards so that their reaction would not affect me adversely. My sister, Andrea, accompanied me, and remained behind to deal with any questions that would be forthcoming.

February 5, 1995

Dear Mom and Dad,
I wish that I did not have to write this letter because
it is going to cause you so much pain. Carl did not
die of cancer, he died from complications related to
AIDS. I have contracted the virus from him and so
I am ill and I don't know how long I have to live.
Please understand that even though my marriage
ended so terribly it does not mean it was not
satisfying. I had a good marriage and Carl treated
me very well, but he was human and so he made
mistakes. I want you to know that nothing you did
in bringing me up, or later in our relationship
contributed in any way to what has happened to me.
I see this as an unfortunate part of life, something
that I have to live with and accept. I will try to do
my best for the children until I am no longer here.
I know that the God that you both serve will help
you through the pain of this disclosure and through
whatever else lies ahead. The faith you have will
sustain you. I love you both.

Rosie

I referred to contracting HIV as 'an unfortunate part
of life'. Those words did not convey the feelings of
personal failure that were with me on that day. To
transfer these burdens to your parents was something I
hated to do. Self doubt and the recriminations plagued
my thoughts. No one wants to inflict pain on anyone,

especially on people whom you love and who love you.

I remember Andrea saying to me when I read the two letters to her, Rena and Len that the shock was so great that her reasoning and understanding were diminished. While she understood from the letters that Carl died from complications connected with AIDS, it took some time for her to assimilate that I had the virus too. Rena and Len were in total disbelief. Probably, because they lived in Florida, they were not privy to any of the rumours linking HIV to Carl and me. Therefore the information was new to Rena and so alien to her that she wanted to scream, but the screams were only heard inside her head. For Len, it was the sadness he remembered. The sadness hung in the room and enveloped them all.

W'EN BETTA CYAAN BE DONE, MEK WORSE TEK OVA

When enduring a difficult situation, which you are powerless to change, brace yourself

MY PLANNED DISCLOSURES NOW COMPLETE, I decided that I was going to focus on my health and try to be proactive. I had put on a lot of weight and I was secretly concerned because I thought something had gone wrong with my metabolism. Most of my friends and relatives were happy with the way I looked; there were no obvious signs of the HIV and to them that meant one thing: that I was well. My friends Lana and Carmen were strong proponents of alternative medicine and they were trying to nudge me along that path.

Before I did anything else, I needed to know my present health status. In October 1996, I called Dr Barry at the pathology department of the University Hospital. I asked him about my T-cell counts during 1992 from tests I had done when Carl was alive. He told me that I was not to worry about the past but that he would personally arrange for me to take the blood test now. At the time, Norma lived in Norbrook which was close to where Dr Barry lived. We arranged that early one morning before he went to work, I was to go up to Norma's and he would meet us there and take the blood sample. I was grateful for the convenience as I was trying to minimize the chatter.

I did not hear from Dr Barry on the day he promised me the results. Norma and Shelly were in daily contact with me, so they were anxious to know the results. I finally got Dr Barry on the phone.

'I tried unsuccessfully to contact you for several days now; and by the way how are you today?'

'I've been pretty busy, under a lot of stress.'

'Sorry to hear that but you know why I am calling. I am anxious to know my T-cell count. I always thought it was good but when I did not hear from you promptly I started to be concerned.' There was an ominous silence, and my heart rate quickened.

'To tell you the truth Mrs Stone, I thought it would have been better than it is. Your T-cell count is 50.'

'Fifty, what do you mean – as in 5 and a 0.'

'Yes but the plus side is, you are feeling well and looking good. We can do further investigations. I will give Dr Grace a call and you should too and we will decide the best way forward.'

'Wow, I did not know that one could have such a low count and not be in the hospital. I thought there would be physical manifestations of a 50 T-cell count. I do not remember Carl's count getting that low. This virus is really something else; it affects everyone differently. Anyway, goodbye Dr Barry, thanks for everything you do for me I'll certainly be calling on you again.'

'Anytime. You know I will help and support you in all the ways that I can.'

I called Shelly immediately. We talked for quite some time about how shocked we both were about the 50 T-cell count. We had tickets for the Ward Theatre in downtown Kingston, that evening to attend a piano recital by Oswald Russell. As we watched and listened to the performance, I thought we were definitely not what we seemed to be. Our exterior conceals so much of who we are. My HIV infection, my 50 T-cell count all had roots in and was born of our physical love. One of life's most palatable fruits made bitter by Carl's misdeeds. I contemplated the reality of my 50 T-cells to everyone else's 1,000. I started to feel uncomfortable. My compromised immune system was at a huge disadvantage, surrounded as I was by hundreds of theatre patrons and millions of germs just ready to attack. I breathed deeply to quiet my mind. My eyes were seeing the stage again. I had to drag my thoughts there too.

Reluctantly, I was attentive to the music for a few seconds, and then a silent unease began to spread through my body. I felt it travel from my neck rippling slowly down, past my waist to my toes. I suddenly experienced self-consciousness; as if everyone at the Ward Theatre could see my feelings and guess that I hardly had any T-cells left. I was brought back to the performance which was intended to be a relaxing and enjoyable experience by the standing ovation for Oswald by some of the patrons.

Shelly came by my home later. The first thing she wanted to do was to call Dr Barry again and make sure that I had heard the correct number. I did and it was confirmed again: my T-cell count was 50.

'Rosie, have you called Dr Grace? How did she react?'
'As calm and professional as ever. I have an appointment with her, she is going to look at the results in detail and talk to me about them.'

'Rosie, where did you get the idea that your T-cell count was between 600 and 800? Did you get a paper with it written down? Did Dr Barry or Dr Grace tell you these numbers? You could not have pulled them from a hat, could you?'

'Very funny Shelly, I do not think it was as arbitrary as that, but I honestly can't remember. Someone must have given me the impression, some doctor I mean must have mentioned 800 that is the number I remember.'

'Eight hundred is not an impression it is a concrete number. Let's go back and try to solve this mystery especially in light of your suspicion that Dr Barry was not forthcoming with your results from 1992.'

'You know that I do not think they have done anything unethical or wrong. They are just trying to protect me. They answered my questions and queries and they were all about Carl; he was the one that was seriously ill.'

'Can you try to jog your memory? Where did you do your first HIV test?'

'In Dr Grace's office after they found out that Carl was HIV positive.'

'Did you get the results from that test?'

'Yes, that I was HIV positive too. All the other tests Carl and I did at the same time at the Ripple building at the University Hospital.'

'Did you get the results of those tests?'

'Oh my God, I never asked. I thought I was fine. My only complaint was fatigue. I cannot believe that I did not ask. Now it almost seems negligent. To be truthful I never considered any of this until this moment.'

'It is quite understandable given the circumstances you

were dealing with. I recall asking you directly about your T-cell count and you were quite confident in your reply. That was just a few months after Carl died. It was around that time that the doctor took you off AZT.'

'I was so elated to be off of that dreadful medicine that made me so ill. I also had total confidence in Dr Grace. I think she told me that they did not see a significant enough benefit in relation to its ill effects on me. My inference from all of this was that I was OK, at least for a while.'

'Well your "while" is over. You had three years of relatively good health. We have to find solutions to the present problem. I think you should ask about your history so that you can have an idea if your counts were always stable or if over time they gradually came down.'

'There is also the evolving standards of the medical profession as to when to treat AIDS with medication. We have to keep in mind that in 1992–1993 the doctors were still divided on when to start giving HIV patients medication. There were some that came down on the side of treatment very soon after knowledge of infection. There were others who considered waiting until the patient presented some related illness.'

'There is also the controversy as to when an HIV-positive person moves into the category of having AIDS. Some in the profession use T-cell count; if a patient's count falls below 200 then one is categorized as having AIDS. Still others require an HIV/AIDS-related illness to occur before a patient is put in that grouping.'

'Oh my! Even though I have not had even the flu for

over five years, I would still be said to have AIDS. What to do about this 50 T-cells is beyond me. I do not want to live with this kind of dread hanging over me. If the signs of HIV were evident it would be easier to do something about them but to now consciously go again on medication to be sick is so very hard to contemplate.'

'I think you should talk to Dr Grace who is in a better position than I am to help you make a decision.'

'Shelly, I have been reading a lot of books on the virus and I am considering some kind of alternative medicine. Of course I believe I have the luxury of mulling over these ideas because I don't feel sick yet. Incidentally, I was looking at this before I got this 50 T-cell result. What do you think?'

'I am not averse to any method that you think will help; but I do not know enough about the alternatives to offer any judgment on them.'

'I'll talk to Dr Grace about my options.'

Mr Nelson came to me well recommended by my friend Carmen. She made the appointment for me. He seemed to have an assortment of knowledge, including a great deal of experience in treating cancer. He was offering to remove toxins that were harmful to my body and to strengthen my immune system. After meeting with him I realized that two issues I was trying to avoid by staring clear of conventional medicine were now staring me in the face. Money and medication, these twin pillars to my very existence. I would have to wrestle with them no matter which course I chose.

The alternate path that Mr Nelson was offering me

was very pricey. It was even quoted in United States dollars. This was going to be difficult for me. I was not ready to take money that I had earmarked for Tricia and Timothy's education and divert it to medicine that would not even guarantee my health. I could also detect a potential problem with Mr Nelson in relation to my attitude to taking medicine. He believed that the more averse I was to taking these drugs, the harder it would be for me. I was therefore in dire straits. My experience in taking AZT had been problematic. I had been sick every single day and therefore I was not looking forward to putting my body and mind through that agony. Mr Nelson believed I was putting up psychological barriers that would not help me in the healing process. I was in a lot of trouble even before I began.

Over the next couple of weeks I talked in depth individually with friends Carmen and Lana who were pro the alternative path. Norma and Shelly were sceptical; they did not know Mr Nelson and were as unsure of what to do as I was. I read books, I listened to tapes, and I did all I could to ensure that I made a decision that was mine and that was as informed as it could be. Mr Nelson gave me a plan to change some of my eating habits and to restart my exercise programme, that had become neglected.

Carl had been dead for a little over three years. Since then I had tried going to the gym with Andrea, but my energy levels were down and I was sometimes terrified that I would faint or pass out and cause a spectacle. I saw women whispering and I knew they were whispering about me. I had all kinds of fears. Some of these fears I shared with friends and my sisters.

Acquaintances came up to me and asked about my health. I had overheard women talking about me in the changing room of the gym, so I never went in that room again. Shelly and I discussed these fears at length. We spoke about irrational fears and real fears. Shelly cautioned me to be careful not to get caught up in fears that were not rooted in fact. While I knew that I could not allow these fears to define my life, I was sure some of them were real. The day that I heard that a HIV-positive man had been asked to leave another gym because the other members were upset about his sweat, I knew that I was not going back to another gym in Jamaica. I would have to find a gym instructor that I could trust and who would not be afraid of me or my HIV.

Carmen decided that she was going to help me with my exercise regimen. She came for me at 4:45 a.m. three times a week and we walked at the Mona dam. I was a bit apprehensive at first. After a couple of days I felt comfortable with Carmen, knowing that she would protect me and if a crisis occurred she could handle the contingencies. She was also very good at reading when I was able to do a little more and when I was tired. Along with exercising, I started eating in a new way, and began to lose some of the excess weight I had gained. I started to feel better about how I looked, but my energy levels were not normal. I could not have walked on two successive days. My body needed time to recover. We walked Monday, Wednesday and Friday mornings, and I had to sleep for at least two solid hours or more after each walk. I did this for several months.

In the interim I had made the leap of faith in going with Mr Nelson on the alternative pathway. It involved so much. Rodakem were individual sealed vials of a clear substance. One had to be taken before breakfast each morning. Rodakem was designed to boost the immune system. Then there was the Shark Cartilage that came in a powder form. I had to mix and drink this daily. There were at least three different sets of medication. They were in capsule form, some large, some small, which also had to be taken every day. There were capsules for night-time use. They did not make me sick to the stomach like AZT, they were just difficult to take, especially the ones that I had to drink. I retched my way from one dose to the other. Integral to Mr Nelson's plan were a series of colonics; he was going to supply the board and the attachments so that I would be able to do colonics at home.

As expected, my body had problems dealing with some of the medication. After taking one particular capsule all the muscles on my back would go into spasms. The pain would be unbearable and it would not ease for a long time. Norma and Andrea were both upset by the pain that I was in. They went to Mr Nelson to get some antidote to relieve it. Apparently I was allergic to something in the capsule he had made especially for me. I had to return that set of capsules to Mr Nelson. There were some medicines that I could not manage visually much less take them into my body.

In January of 1997 Phillip's father died and I decided that I would attend the funeral. Sharon, a close friend of Phillip and Lisa – she had helped me at the Third

World concert when Carl got ill – volunteered to take Andrea and me. In the church, Andrea sat in the back, while I sat with Sharon near a fan, because I sometimes felt a little bothered when I got hot. I was listening intently to the sermon, close to the end of the service, when without warning I realized that I was not feeling myself and that I was going to faint. I remember thinking, *not here, please not here. I have to fight this feeling, stay upright.* I remember not being able to hear the sounds around me, but I clenched my teeth and my fists as tightly as I could to give me strength not to fall. I hoped that the feeling would pass quickly, before anyone noticed. I felt Sharon move from beside me and I thought, *I am definitely going to tilt to that side and I might fall.* I was still trying to fight this terrible feeling. As suddenly as it had come, though, the darkness lifted, and I looked up to see Andrea beside me. I moved myself upright, as I had indeed tilted to the side that Sharon had vacated. The person to my left had noticed and moved to give me space to lie down on the bench. I managed to squeeze out a smile and whisper that I was OK. Andrea asked me if I wanted to go now and I answered yes. As I left the church, concerned friends asked if I could make it to the car. I did.

My body had the strength to get me there, but I felt as if I had run a marathon. I was sweating profusely. Beads of perspiration had formed on my face and all over my body, and I tried to cool down in Sharon's air-conditioned car.

'I am so sorry to be the cause of all this commotion.'
'That's OK. How are you feeling?'
'The faint came so quickly I could do nothing about it.

I feel depleted.'

'Do you have any idea what might have precipitated this?'

'I have some ideas,' said Andrea who had been quiet so far, 'I don't know if they are correct, but Rose did too much this morning. I also think that a funeral would not be a place I would go to now if I were in her position.'

'I go with how I feel and I felt fine,' I said. 'The only thing I did that was unusual was that I got an injection from a doctor, I can't remember his name but it has to do with the alternate path that I am on.'

'That is what I mean Rose, you have so much going on, it is really a lot for you. I do not think that you should have gone up to the front to greet the family. And you did it in your style, which is hurriedly. I think it was too much for you to manage.'

'Whatever the cause I was scared out of my mind. When I looked at Rosie and saw her eyes roll over in her head and her rigid body, I just thought, I have to get Andrea. I can't manage this. I thought it was very serious.'

'In my defence, if you had not gotten up, I would not have tilted.'

'I could not know that, Rosie.'

'To be truthful, neither could I, but I came out of the faint just in time. The lady to my left was just about to lay me prostrate. She probably thought I was dying.'

'I thought so too. It was really scary. Another thing, Andrea, I was surprised to see Rosie recover in the few seconds it took for me to get you around the back. Not only were you calm, but also you knew right away that she could walk from that church. I was so glad you were there, I really was.'

'I suppose that is experience. I looked at her and she said she could walk. She still had her wits about her. I could see that she could make it to the car.'

Over the next week I tried without success to find out the cause of my fainting spell. After speaking with Mr Nelson, I decided that I would not take any more of the injections just in case my system was not tolerating them well. Apart from this isolated incident in January, the year 1997 was shaping up to be a good one. I was feeling and looking better than I had in a couple of years. A packaged trip was being planned from Jamaica to Trinidad that was a part of the Indian cricket tour of the West Indies. I started to make plans to attend.

April 1997

I was making great progress as far as my diet and exercise programme were concerned. Lana introduced me to a product from Canada called Clean and Harmony that would help to remove parasites and toxins from the body. We talked about it and it seemed easy to take and it was a short-term course: I would only take it for one week. I started taking the tablets on Sunday of the week that I was to go on the cricket trip to Trinidad. I walked with Carmen on the Monday morning. On Wednesday when she called at 4:30 a.m., I told her that I was not feeling very well, I was a little tired so I would not walk until I came back from cricket. I thought it best to rest for the remainder of the week because I was leaving on Friday. By Thursday, Carmen and Andrea became concerned and they tried talking me out of going on the trip to Trinidad. I would not hear any of it because I really thought I was just a bit worn out and that going to cricket, something that I loved to do, was what I needed. On Friday morning Andrea called me from work to convince me to reconsider.

'Rose, I think that you should not go on this trip.'

'I appreciate your concern, Andrea, but so many things have been taken away from me. I want to go. I think I will be all right.'

'You have not been out of bed for two full days. Does that sound to you like you are in good shape to travel?'

'I was thinking about that. The travel time is quite long, so I plan on sleeping all the way and then I will be ready for cricket.'

'Rose do you think you can manage this all by yourself?'

'Remember, I did it already. I went to a test match in Antigua and even though I had a minor problem, it all worked out.'

'I would not call staying up all night in Antigua with ice on your forehead with Norma giving you moral support at this end in Jamaica a minor problem.'

'I would not wilfully endanger myself.'

'That is part of the problem: you are not seeing yourself. I am not the only one that is concerned. Your friends have been calling me – Carmen in particular.'

'I hope you are wrong on this because that would mean I am in a bad place. Tricia is taking me to buy two pairs of jeans for the trip, so we have to leave a little early.'

'The buying of the jeans at the last minute should tell you Rose that something is not right about this trip. Usually those jeans would have been bought before today. I feel very unsettled about all of it.'

'The store is on the way to the airport. That's why we are going there right now. I will talk to you from the car.'

I did not have the unsettling feeling that Andrea felt. I did feel tired but it did not alarm me in any way. Tricia and I bought the jeans and headed for the airport. I noticed that the British West Indies counter looked deserted. I looked at my ticket for the first time since it was dropped off. I had asked Tricia to give me the time when I should check-in at the airport. Instead she had given me the departure time. The flight had already taken off. I was now too tired to be disappointed. I called Andrea at work.

'I missed the flight Andrea.'

'Thanks to Jehovah, I am so happy. How are you feeling?'

'Not so good. I am very tired. You were probably right I could not pull up my zipper.'

'Your zipper, what happened to your zipper?'

'When I went to buy the jeans I had to ask Tricia to pull it up for me.'

'The jeans were too tight?'

'No I did not have the strength to pull up the zipper.' I started to cry, overwhelmed by emotion and thoughts of what could have happened if I had gotten on the plane.

'I realized that I did not look at the ticket because I did not have the energy.' I was still crying.

'Rose, do not cry. Things will work out.'

I went home that Friday and slept intermittently all day. By Saturday morning Andrea had gone on field service early and she called me at about nine o'clock to find out how I was. The conversation was very brief.

'Rose are you feeling any better?'

'No, worse.'

'The kind of worse that you want me to come home?'

'Yes.'

Andrea came home that day and she did not leave my side for the next three weeks. My body became one whole organ of discomfort and disrepair. One of the first things I asked Andrea to promise me was that she would not allow me to be taken to any hospital in Jamaica. The second was that Dr Grace would not be called unless I had a temperature. Over the next couple of days I got weaker. I tried to lift my foot to step in the bath and I was unable to do so not only because I was weak, but also my motor functions were impaired. Andrea said she would sponge me down in bed. Many things happened to me over the following 10 to 14 days of which I have no memory.

I remembered knowing that I was not well and thinking that it must be related to HIV/AIDS. Thoughts began to swim in and out of my mind. These thoughts did not stay with me for long. It seemed they came to me in a dream. I also remember the word *comatose* and wondered if that could describe my state and thought that if it did it was OK because my body in that state would heal itself and I would recover. My whole body was itching. I tried to get a little comfort by moving beneath the sheets but I could hardly do that. Mr Nelson came to see me early on Saturday before the cloud descended over me. He wanted to take me to a clinic in Tijuana, Mexico that he was attached to but the price was prohibitive and even though there was some discussion about it I knew I was not going. I remember Mr Nelson and Carmen talking about colonics, so the thought of colonics floated in and out of my dream state and I wanted to get strong just to have the colonics.

I recall having severe back pains and indicating to Andrea that she rub Mineral Ice on it for me. As she put the rub on my back I started to scream and cry in agony. Andrea was startled and took my top off. She too started to cry. Unbeknownst to Andrea or me, I had been scratching my back and large welts were there and elsewhere over my body.

Days and nights merged. I was in the bathroom on one of my good days, trying to wash my hands, and I happened to look in the mirror. I was horrified at what I saw. My face was swollen so large it seemed it would burst. My eyes were blood red. I whispered to Andrea 'You cannot allow our parents to see me like this, they are going to hurt too much.'

They never did.

I am aware some times that I have stopped talking. I have stopped talking because I do not have the energy. It takes too much out of me. After about four days I talk with my eyelids shut. It takes too much energy to open them. My friends are visiting me around the clock. I sense their affection, and in some their panic. I imagine that Andrea must be going through a lot with my friends; with everybody giving her suggestions. I feel Carmen's presence and I know she spends long hours visiting with me. Andrea feeds me as both strength and coordination have deserted me. I struggle to eat and sleep but I am aware of this only because Andrea is always encouraging me to try to eat a little more and she tells me I am not sleeping. I do not feel the deprivation of any of it.

Andrea tells me it is time to call Dr Grace as my temperature has gone up. When the doctor arrives she tells me she is very upset with me for the delay in calling her. Dr Lois, a dermatologist who is a friend of Shelly, came soon after. I get antibiotics and all kinds of topical creams and ointments. I recall saying a lot of 'thank you very much, thank you very much.' I do not know if I am saying this at appropriate times and I wonder if I should stop saying it. As soon as I make up my mind to stop saying that phrase, I say it again and again. I hope the doctors and my friends do not think I am losing my mind because it seems they are the only words that are coming out of my mouth.

I have a sense that the doctors come to see me again but I am not sure. Lana comes to see me and I remember. She takes one look at me and says to Andrea, 'Andy, this calls for prayers', and they leave the room together. I try to find in my memory if Lana came to see me before but I get more exhausted just trying. Another memory is of two strangers visiting me. They talk a lot. I do not recall if I take part in the conversation. They tell me about a doctor in Miami that they had both gone to and they think he might be able to help. He has helped other Jamaicans and I should try to see him. As I listen to the two men I begin to see the possibility of going to Miami. The only problem is that I am so weak I do not know if I can travel. I have not left my room in weeks. I try to think about how it might work, but it seems impossible so I try to turn off my mind. That is very difficult for me. I seem to dwell in my mind. *I inhabit it very well. It is the only place that I exist. I am perfectly at ease there. I can think about many varied subjects but then I must let them go. If I do not try very hard to remember I will be all right.*

Carmen talks to me about giving me an enema and she does. I have a vague recollection of her carrying me to do colonics, but I don't know if it went well. I believe it can help me to get a little better. While I don't remember the actual colonics I recall the lady letting us sit and rest in her living room for a time because I am so tired. Shelly and Norma I see often but I don't converse with them. I also recall Shelly taking me to the lab at Medical Associates and a technician coming to the car to take the sample from me for a blood test. I just cannot make it inside. A more abiding image is of Carmen cutting off the excess skin from the soles of my feet. Every day my skin sheds some more.

I get ready to go to Miami to see the doctor. There are no images of how I prepared myself for this trip but I know I am travelling with Peter who is Shelly's husband. He is travelling on the Memorial weekend and says I can accompany him. I seem to have forgotten going to the airport, checking in, going through customs and even boarding the plane. What I recall is that I am very uncomfortable in my own skin. I am cold. I am hot. I feel I am not going to make it to the doctor. I am horrified by the thought of going through Customs and Immigration in Florida because I believe that they will know that I am infected with HIV and deny me entry to see the doctor. I know of at least one person that this had happened to. All through the flight I express my fears to Peter and he gently tries to calm me with words of assurance and comfort. He reminds me that he would help me with everything. I am just to stay close to him and we will get through. The tears start as I struggle for control and strength. I do not remember the trauma of the airport but I recall the relief I feel in seeing my sister Rena and her husband Len. I start to sob as I get in the car. I am totally exhausted and emotionally spent.

Over the next couple of weeks I slowly came to the realization that I had started to inhabit my body again. I had started to know what I felt. Visiting Dr Corklin Steinhart certainly helped in this regard. He did a blood test when I visited his offices. Later I returned to see him and he explained the results. He told me about viral load. I had heard and read about one's viral load but mine was never done because that test was not available in Jamaica. My viral load was in the 3,000 range. He explained that it meant that there were many copies of the virus in my system. I would always have the virus in me, but with medication the viral load could be reduced and become undetectable, at below 500 copies. The T-cell count was beyond belief. It was now two. The enormity of this was nearly beyond my comprehension. Dr Steinhart was realistic but optimistic about the triple therapy medication that were now on the market. It involved three types of medication working in tandem to attack the virus. He suggested Viracept, a protease inhibitor and two anti-virals, Zerit and Epivir. I would take these together with an antibiotic and other more common drugs to counteract the side effects of the main drugs.

The medication was costly: US$1,400 converted to Jamaican dollars every month represented to me the use of money that I had earmarked for my children's education; J$40,000 a month for drugs that might not work and that were certain to cause major problems to my body's system was reason for a lot of thought. When I voiced this concern to Dr Steinhart, he offered to save for me returned medication that his patients brought back to the office. Other members of his staff would also try to do the same. I wondered out loud if I had any options. If I did not take the medication, I asked, what was likely to happen to me? He explained that once you have contracted HIV, your immune system gets compromised. The fact that I had a T-cell count of two was the significant factor. The cause was not as critical as the result. What was important was to try to get the viral load lower and the T-cell count higher and I would begin to feel better. The only option he had to offer me was the medication.

As I sat in that office in May 1997, I thought about the issue of life and death. The more rational thought suggested that I was already too far gone down the road to death, and that path seemed significantly easier. I could will my way back to the other 'half-way land' that I existed in so easily just a couple of weeks before. There was no pain or expectation in that hazy state. The more irrational thought process told me that there were other people and issues greater than self that needed to be brought to the forefront of any such deliberation. These decisions were probably not in my realm of control any way. I could choose to take the medication and still die. As I pondered I spoke to Dr Steinhart about my children and how difficult their father's death and my illness had been on them. Even though I recognized that for my children I had to take the medication, I still wrestled with the decision. I rebelled against the injustice of Carl's misdeeds retaining a stranglehold on my life choices.

As I left Dr Steinhart's office I contemplated how my life was going to change even further. A life made up entirely of efforts to survive HIV/AIDS and the onslaught of disease; a life revolving around taking at least 15 tablets a day. I knew that they would create havoc on my system. I hoped I could survive with at least part of myself intact. I called my friends in Jamaica to tell them about the T-cell count of two. I think they were as much in awe of this count as I was.

There are no words to describe what the first ten days of taking the HIV drugs did to my body and my psyche. I went to hell on this earth on that first day. My body, already weakened, was severely tested when the drugs entered my system. Everything that could go wrong did. I had difficulty in just swallowing the tablets, especially the Viracept that at the time had no special coating and would dissolve in my mouth before I could swallow it. During those initial days I could barely take half of the quota that the doctor prescribed. I developed an allergic reaction to Imodium. It had to be replaced by Lomotil. Vomiting, diarrhoea and fainting spells became everyday occurrences. While the diarrhoea could be somewhat controlled with medication, the vomiting and fainting spells were relentless. The medication was to be taken after meals, but the meals refused to stay in my stomach. On the first day, the worst, I fainted at least 20 times.

The miracle of modern medicine enabled me to leave Florida by the middle of June. I felt strong enough to lift a bag from a carousel at the Norman Manley International airport in Jamaica and on that same day accompany my son to the doctor (he had developed the symptoms of chicken pox while on the flight with me). I travelled again in late August and went to see Dr Steinhart. My T-cell count had climbed to 80 and my viral load was on its way down. I had started once again to feel a little better. I was no longer a spectator to my life. I moved from observing it through an opaque glass to participation with self-doubts and intense fatigue. Instead of glimpsing through the glass I was enveloped in a haze of despair.

In October of that year I would be 50 years old. Shelly insisted on celebrating my birthday. She thought there was plenty to be pleased about and to give thanks for. She was inviting friends, some of whom had not seen me recently. I decided to use this opportunity to thank them for their steadfastness.

I include this tribute to my friends as it speaks to my state of mind on the evening of October 8, 1997.

> *In a few hours I will be celebrating another milestone in my life. I would like you all to share in my celebration of life by focusing on a few hurdles that I overcame in the year 1996–1997.*
>
> *In the latter part of August I told my children Timothy and Tricia that their father died of AIDS and that I had contracted the disease from him. I sought professional guidance as to the timing of the revelation to them, but in retrospect I don't think there was ever a good time to say this to one's children. Tricia in particular had just lost her US visa, and I think now that this disclosure*

marked the beginning of loss of parental control of both my children. Timothy redoubled his efforts to find his birth mother and I tried very hard to keep the family together as the stress strained the cords that bound us together.

I also made a similar revelation to my parents and my brothers. My dad stared at me in unbelief as I started to read a letter I had written to them in 1995. He said, and I quote 'Rose why are you repeating those terrible things about Carl, you mustn't do that.' After I left he sat motionless for many hours trying to digest what I had told him. My mother's grief was undeniable. My brothers were silent. They looked at me as if I was from another planet. I don't know if you can imagine being in my shoes and probably I should not ask you to, but I don't know which was harder to execute, telling my parents or telling my children.

Further disclosures were made to many friends, many of you who are here tonight. Not all disclosures went smoothly and they were a few that were more traumatic than others, for this I apologize. This was not my intention.

For the first time since I was diagnosed with AIDS, I got very ill. I want to use the occasion to thank all of you who played a part in my recovery. For the flowers, for the visits, for the kisses, for the prayers and touches I couldn't feel, for the massaging of my feet, for all the loving thoughts – I will be eternally grateful. I also wish to reassure many of my friends than I definitely looked worse than I felt, probably because the memory of those three weeks has left me entirely.

For those who have been a part of my life for this

past year, know that these four hurdles were just four of many that I had to face during this particular year. I would like to say thank you to a few people.

To my friends who are present here tonight, to those whom could not make it – in particular, Donna – to my absent Jehovah's Witness friends, all of whom encouraged me, cried with me, were joyous when the results were good, I do appreciate all of this.

To Carmen – my most compassionate friend, my friend whom I felt safe to walk around the dam with because I knew she would protect me if any unforeseen thing occurred. She was never afraid to touch me at any time and this speaks volumes to her compassion.

To Shelly and Peter as a couple – thank you for always making me comfortable on our trips to Europe and everywhere that we interacted.

To John who knew from the onset and was the friend who provided the male perspective in the plight in which I had found myself, and who was always there for me.

To my dear friend Norma who was my backbone during those early years. She provided just the right kind and amount of love, support, and understanding that I needed.

To my soulmate Shelly. Your irreverent humour was and is just what I need to provide the counter to this horrible predicament. I can always depend on Shelly to find humour in the most unlikely place. I can share with her my innermost thoughts when it comes to the harsh side of AIDS and know that I will always be buffered by her humour. We talked about the AIDS shuffle; we fantasized about the shirts to shock people, with HIV on the front and the plus sign on the back. When my T-cell count went down to two she was as horrified as when it was

*at 50 but then a t-shirt with a big TWO on it helped to
ease the pain. Shelly's own brand of humour has indeed
been a balm to my psyche. Her love and support cannot
be questioned.*

*To Andrea, Rena and Len, who are not here tonight –
the only thing that needs to be said is that I would not be
here if they were not part of my life. I will never forget
the six hours of pure hell that they endured with me
when I first started taking my medication.*

*Along with HIV came the loss of friendships, the
myriads of problems, the periods of self-doubt. It also
meant the strengthening and deepening of friendships,
the solving of problems and the unmistakable well of
strength I think that only comes from this kind of distress.
There is still wonder and amazement at the things that
are still possible given the constraints of this disease and
amazingly there is still hope, there is still joy.*

After reading this tribute aloud at the party and
talking with those present I was amazed at how much I
had forgotten about my recent scare. I realized that
some of my friends had thought that I was going to die
when they saw me earlier in May. Lisa could barely
look at me now because it upset her that my eyes were
red, my face was discoloured, and I had lost so much
weight. My friends had stories about those three weeks
that I needed to hear. I decided to speak to Andrea
and to Shelly to get their perspective on the ordeal
that we all endured.

'Andrea, did you think I was going to die?'

'Personally, no, I did not. I couldn't and wouldn't allow
myself the time to think that. I asked Dr Grace, who

wanted to put you in the hospital, if there was anything the hospital could do that I could not do and she said no. She prescribed double strength antibiotics for you and arranged for some blood tests to be done. Dr Lois, your dermatologist, also prescribed antibiotic creams for you. I spoke to both of them and asked if there was anything else that they could do for you. Their answer was no. My next question was, so what are you saying? Their response was silence. At that point I knew what was not being said. I probably did think of you dying at that point but did not allow the thought to stay with me. What did stay however was extreme anxiety and feelings of knots in my stomach at all times.'

'How long after I got sick did you call the doctor?'

'Exactly one week.'

'Oh, I did not realize it was so soon. Can you describe what my symptoms were?'

'OK let me list them: One – you were extremely weak. You did however get up to go to the bathroom. Two – your eyes were always closed even though you were not sleeping. Even when you went to the bathroom you kept your eyes closed. Only once did you open them and looked in the mirror. Three – you hardly ate any food. You did however drink a lot of water with glucose and sometimes with two drops of a liquid called Recovery that Mr Nelson had given you. Four – you did not speak much, however if you were asked a question you would answer. Five – you developed a temperature which, by about the sixth day, had risen to what I thought was a frightening level. The double strength antibiotic from Dr Grace brought down your temperature as soon you started taking them. Six – you lost weight. It seemed to me you just lay there and lost a lot of weight during the first week. Seven – and then there was the peeling of your skin.'

'Which part of my body was peeling?'

'Every part of your body was peeling, from your face to the soles of your feet. The worse parts were your feet and your face. Thick pieces of skin from your feet would fall off. Sometimes pieces would be hanging off which had to be cut. Carmen would come everyday and deal with that. Sometimes she spent over an hour dealing with just your feet. I really don't know how to describe your face. The whole top layer of your skin, which, by this time, looked damaged, was peeling. While what was below was smooth and free of blemish it did have a look of rawness, tenderness, and discomfort even though you did not express any such feeling about it. The creams from Dr Lois slowly helped your face to start looking normal again. At one point your whole body started itching you. With what little strength you had you tried to relieve this by rubbing your body on the bed sheets. You dealt with your face with more intensity. You used a dry rag to constantly scratch your face. You also complained that your face felt as if it was on fire. I wanted you to stop using the rag because I thought it contributed to this but you said the itching was too intense and unbearable.'

'Isn't it amazing that I could go through all of this and be completely oblivious to it?'

'Maybe it had something to do with the fact that all this time your eyes were closed.'

'Very funny Andrea. How many friends came to visit me and did I speak to them?'

'I cannot tell you how many but they were a lot. Norma, Shelly and Carmen came each day, sometimes two or three times per day depending on how long they spent. Many times they stayed all day. At first when your other friends visited you they were hesitant to speak to you because you were so still in the bed and your eyes were closed. They only spoke to me and then they whispered. I think I was a little bit angry with them even though I did not show it. I told them to speak to you because you could respond to them. They did this and you would converse with them.'

'Did anyone give you advice as to what to do for me?'

'Yes. I really cannot remember who did but I remember what advice was given and I remember who did not try to enforce anything. Shelly and Norma at no time tried to tell me dos and don'ts they just went along with me, they made it so easy. Carmen was good too. She would do so much for you and would always ask and tell me what she was going to do. She would always speak to you first. Then there were the ones who thought what your diet should be. I had to tell them that some of the food you did not like. They would insist. It was only after I told them that even though you looked the way you looked you would refuse any food you did not like, that they stopped.'

'Was Lisa here? She spoke as if she was.'

'Yes Rosie, she was. So were Sharon, Candy, and Sheryl.'

'I don't remember any of them being here.'

'Well they were, and you even talked with them sometimes.'

'I vaguely remember two men visiting me. I do

remember that they spoke a lot.'

'But you spoke a lot too. It was the first time you sat up in bed in three weeks and spoke to anyone. I remember that during the conversation there was a lot of laughter especially coming from you. In fact outside of Carmen, Shelly and Norma you spoke the most to them. You even went down the stairs and saw them out. I was so surprised and happy. You actually were able to get out of bed and walk through your door down the stairs and back up again, all of this without help from anyone. I even remarked to them about this fact.'

'That's so amazing, and I don't remember.'

'I don't understand because we made such a big issue out of it.'

'How did you handle Mama and Daddy? They must have been upset that they could not see me.'

'You can be sure that Mom was upset. I told her on the phone when I knew that she suspected that something was not right. I told her that you had asked that they not visit for now and she seemed to take it in stride at least to me because she was thinking of not adding to my stress level. I was glad that you made that decision. The day she did come, when Barry brought her, was nearly three weeks after you had been in bed. I was cutting the excess skin from around your fingernails. Lisa, Norma and Shelly were here that day. I could see the pain that she was in. She had told me politely the day before she came that if her child died and she did not see her, she did not know how she could take it. In any case I was just holding out that you could look a little better.'

'I don't remember how many times Carmen took me

to do colonics but somewhere in my hazy mind I did not think they worked.'

'I do not know how many times you went but I think Norma took you once when Carmen was unable to take you. Carmen told me it worked well and she was very happy that you were able to muster the strength to go. She believed it helped you enormously. I remember your friends wanting to help but I felt comfortable with Norma, Shelly and Carmen because I knew they would not panic if you fainted or anything like that. Another of your friends offered to stay with you while I got a chance to go to a meeting but I had to decline her offer because you did not want to be left with her.'

This is Shelly's account of what happened.

I was extremely sceptical of the 'alternative treatments', and even shared some irreverent remarks with Norma about the 'AFF' at the end of the practitioner's name. However, I had no answers myself and would have been supportive of any treatment that would help Rosie and that she would be comfortable with. Rosie herself, was very well informed and availed herself of varied and detailed information, regarding all aspects of the disease, including scientific data.

Not being around Rosie as much as Andrea, I did not realize the fragile state of health she was in at the time of the planned Trinidadian trip, I was only happy that she was going to do something she enjoyed very much. Ever the avid sporting fan, Rosie has certainly tried to acquaint me with the nuances of the game of cricket, largely unsuccessfully, and I have always been quite amazed at the passion she has for it. In this case, there seems to have been a self-correcting mechanism, or very good fortune that her poor health and general lack of energy ultimately caused her to miss the flight. The part that I found most incredible and could not help chiding my friend about, was that she was willing to get on a flight, not being able to pull up her zipper.

The descent into the abyss that was to become her home for three weeks was very rapid. My memory is of Rosie being in bed with her eyes closed, barely speaking except for little whispers, eating very little, but still being incredibly polite, thanking everyone for every little gesture. On the odd occasion that she opened her eyes, they were blood red, and her skin was literally moulting. I don't recall being afraid that she was dying, and she did not even seem to be experiencing great discomfort, but she was just 'absent', and we all felt very helpless, so we just did what we could. My role was 'mother', so I helped with the planning and food preparation for Tricia's eighteenth birthday party.

On the evening of the party, I went upstairs to see Rosie, still a bit shaken, as I had just heard from a very good friend that a friend of ours, who we had planned to visit, had just died of AIDS. Rosie coincidentally asked about him, and in my confusion, I asked her how she knew he had died. She, of course, was shocked and I was mortified at my insensitivity, but thankfully before long she would not remember any of it. Andrea and I spent the rest of the evening trying to ensure that none of Tricia's friends came up the stairs but that did not stop a particularly brash young lady from bursting through the door.

By the end of the first week, Andrea called in Dr Grace, because Rosie's temperature had gone up. A blood test was ordered, which necessitated Rosie actually leaving not only the bed and bedroom, but also the house. The exercise seemed to take the entire day, although the technician was kind enough to come to the car and take the blood as soon as we got to the hospital. I remember Andrea painstakingly tidying and dressing Rosie, in a pink silk shirt and pants of matching colour, with her hair pinned up and a pair of sunglasses to conceal the crimson eyes. After the dressing was over, Rosie had to rest before being helped down the stairs, to rest again before walking across the living room, and slowly, laboriously to the car. How painfully thin and frail she looked and everything seemed to be happening in slow motion, and we felt as if we were unable to exhale through it all.

There was a point that the skin problem needed attention, and although Rosie was still reluctant to see any doctors at that time, she agreed to Grace's suggestion and allowed me to ask my good friend who was a dermatologist, to see her at home. Dr Lois examined her and wrote her a prescription, but the most important aspect of the visit, was that she insisted that Rosie immediately start treatment, and recommended a doctor in Miami. The visit from Dr Lois may have well saved my friend's life.

MARRIAGE GOT TEET, IT BITE LIKE CRAB

Marriage can have tribulations

MY EXPERIENCE WITH HIV/AIDS has been both life consuming and life altering. At first I was overwhelmed by the reality that Carl was ill and the fact that I knew I would lose him. After he died, I became frenzied in trying to give Tricia, then 13 and Timothy, then 9, the tools that I thought they would need to survive their altered lives. Slowly I became devoted to the idea of living – staying alive for my children even if it meant drinking shark's cartilage. The last nine years have been a mixture of agony and contentment: the sorrow of knowing that so many normal everyday occurrences (like picking up and hugging a friend's or acquaintance's new baby) that people take for granted are now not a part of my life; the pleasure I still get from the love of family and the camaraderie of friends. This exquisite anguish is my new reality.

This reality was brought home to me forcefully when sometime in 2001 I was talking to Christine, who worked at the Jamaica AIDS Support, and I was wondering aloud if there was anything I could do to help. She told me of a mother and her seven-year-old, Howard, who were at the hospice. The mother was very ill but the child was not. The child was not in school as it was Christmas time and schools were closed. I offered to go to the hospice and read with Howard over the holidays. I armed myself with crayons, colouring books and storybooks. The hospice provided a quiet place for Howard and me to read and colour together. We read together in a room within the nurses' station. After going there periodically for a couple of weeks I was told that Christine wanted to talk to me. She told me that there had been an outbreak of tuberculosis at the hospice and they were afraid for my health. Tuberculosis could be dangerous for me, with my immune system weakened by HIV. I was devastated. It was irrational to be so upset by such an incident, but I was. I had felt useful and safe at the hospice, and HIV was now intruding on even something as simple as reading to a child in need of comfort. As a precaution, I had to forgo my visits with Howard.

The new reality of AIDS was what brought me to speak to, cry with and hear dozens of stories over the past ten years. I was particularly interested in stories about married women whose lives had been touched by HIV. The stories of Dina, Dorothy and Megan represent snapshots of their lives at the time they intersected with mine. They portray these three women as they first encountered the virus and their varied reactions and that of their husbands.

Dina

I met Dina over the telephone in late 1997. We liked each other immediately. Our marital experiences were so similar that it was uncanny. We were both married to men who had contracted HIV and we were both infected through sex with our husbands. Dina and I found out in 1992, and both our husbands died in 1993. We both had two children and had to survive the emotional and psychological trauma of telling our children that their parents were ill and that they might die very soon. Despite these similarities, our historical perspectives and personality made our experience of HIV/AIDS, and the way it affected our lives, quite different.

Dina's two children, Sharon and Sheldon, were adults when their father David got sick and died from complications resulting from AIDS. Dina was almost 20 years older than I was when we met in 1997. To be faced with HIV complications and aging at the same time seemed particularly tragic to me, but Dina appeared to live her life effortlessly. Even though she was older than I was, in 1997 she was physically stronger. She was also much more independent. She cooked her own meals, enjoyed looking after her garden and she would even go out by herself to a concert if she had no one to join her. She enjoyed going to the yearly flower shows in Jamaica. She went to plays and movies with old friends or with new friends provided by the partnership programme of the Jamaica AIDS Support. In short, Dina loved life and she tried to live it in the best way she could.

Each year Dina spent some months away from Jamaica with Sharon, in Tulsa, Oklahoma. I knew that the time she spent with her daughter, her son-in-law Byron and her two grandchildren, Paul and Melissa, were among the happiest times of her life. Her grandchildren were a constant source of delight and discovery. They called her Grammy, and after Grammy had been visiting for a while, Paul and Melissa did not want her to leave them to go back to Jamaica. Dina usually called me from Tulsa at least once on each trip to share her joy with me. One year, her voice brimming with love and pride, she told me how well Paul, then six, was doing at tennis and how Melissa who was four, was shaking things up at school by telling her friend Clara that her great-grandmother used to own Melissa's great-grandmother as a slave. Clara was very upset by this and went to ask her grandmother why she had done such a thing. Dina and I shared a chuckle at the way Melissa's mind worked.

She spoke about the books she had read while away, and which ones she was bringing back to Jamaica for me. *Midwives* by Chris Bohjalian was one, as she had seen a discussion of it on television. There was laughter in her voice when she told me that as soon as she came home we would get together and pretend that we were on the Oprah Book Club, and have an insightful discussion of our own.

It was at this discussion of *Midwives* that I told Dina that I had thought about writing a book to share my experiences of HIV/AIDS. I asked if she would consider giving me a formal interview, which I would include in my book. She agreed and the following is a transcript of our 2000 interview.

Interview with Dina (2000)

Rosie: I have spoken to you many times about doing this interview why did you decide to do it now?

Dina: I decided to tell my story because I am a survivor and have survived with this disease for probably more than ten years.

Rosie: What helped you to do this?

Dina: I give credit for my survival to my great faith in God and I believe that He has strengthened me and taken me through some very rough times. I continue to be grateful for having lived this long.

Rosie: What has given you the most difficulty in your quest to survive AIDS with all its permutations?

Dina: One of the most devastating aspects of this disease is the way it impacts on your fundamental faith in God. This is true not only for me individually but also for my family as a whole. When the legacy of a good, normal, average marriage is the death of my husband through AIDS and my own infection and affliction by HIV, it is very difficult to reconcile your belief system with the reality of your life. It is difficult to hold on to God.

Rosie: Have you managed to hold on to your faith?

Dina: Yes I have, but I will tell you a story that relates to my family. Throughout this period, while my faith has been steadfast, my daughter's faith has been severely tested. My daughter Sharon lives in the United States with her husband and my two beloved grandchildren. Anyway I was fortunate enough to be visiting her when winter changed to spring and all the beautiful flowers had just burst out in all their glory. I said to Sharon, 'Oh Sharon, I don't know how anyone could wake up on a morning like this when everything was so bare yesterday and see all this beauty and do not believe in God.' My daughter turned to me and said,

"Mummy, I must tell you that there was a time when I lost my faith. When you got ill and I knew how you had to live I couldn't pray. I couldn't pray for a long time."

Rosie this was very painful for me to hear especially since I was unaware of Sharon's temporary loss of faith and the sad truth was that her father and I caused her such anguish.

Rosie: How do you see the years ahead?

Dina: This is the year 2000 and I am 72 years old this year. I certainly did not conceive that AIDS would complicate growing older. I have six close friends that I have told about my illness but regrettably we are all getting older and other things intrude on friendship.

Rosie: What are some of those infringements?

Dina: One friend, her husband recently had a stroke

so her freedom of movement is significantly curtailed. Another has just migrated. One friend lives in Mandeville and has a lot of personal problems. Still another is head of a hospital and her workload is tremendous. While I am in contact with all these friends there are only two that are more available to me and have been tremendous friends. I just found out that one of the two has not been very well, she has an enlarged liver pressing on her lungs and she has not been breathing properly.

Rosie: This all sounds so gloomy.

Dina: Not at all. It's just life and I have met two nice ladies through the AIDS hospice and we go out together. They have become great friends.

Rosie: What about your sisters – how are those relationships going?

Dina: I have three sisters and I find it painful to talk about the relationship I have with them. They are not hostile; I know that they would be there in a crisis, but sometimes I long to hear from them. I have called them and asked them if it has anything to do with my HIV status and they have replied 'no'. I can't do anymore.

Rosie: Do you get along with your children?

Dina: My two children and I get along very well but we have been through a lot together.

Rosie: How did they react to the HIV news?

Dina: I remember I told them at Christmas time. What a time to tell your children bad news! Sharon would be home at Christmas and I wanted to tell both of them together. Sharon and Sheldon. It was horrible. Sheldon wanted to kill his father.

Rosie: Did Sheldon let his father know how angry he was?

Dina: I don't think he spoke to his father about his anger, but David knew that his son was very upset with him, to put it very mildly. I worry about Sheldon because even though he later went to his father's room when David was dying there were many issues left unresolved.

Rosie: For instance?

Dina: Well, my husband played favourites with his children. He adored Sharon but he gave Sheldon a hard time. I knew that he loved his son but he had a hard time expressing those feelings to Sheldon.

Rosie: From what you have told me it seemed that David had difficulty expressing feelings period.

Dina: I suppose so. You know Rosie, he never once told me that he was sorry or thanked me for looking after him.

Rosie: You have to explain that to me. I don't understand.

Dina: Well, when David started losing weight in 1991–92, he developed what looked like a bad skin rash that did not respond to the normal antibiotic treatment. That's how we ended up at [the office of] your now infamous Dr Andrea, the dermatologist. She did a blood test and thought at first that it might be skin cancer. After further tests cancer was ruled out, so they had to look elsewhere. At that time I was working at the University Hospital, so Dr Andrea and I decided to test for HIV to rule out that possibility. I remember the day that the test came back positive and the lab was abuzz. They wanted to find out who the sample belonged to. We had marked it anonymously so no one had any idea that I was connected to this.

Rosie: What emotions were you going through at that time, can you remember?

Dina: I don't want to remember. I just know it was the most horrible day of my life. The next important event I recall is that we were both at Dr Andrea's office, David and I. I knew that we were both HIV positive. He did not. The plan was that he would go in first and talk to the doctor I would join them afterwards so that we could both talk to the doctor and to each other.

Rosie: So what happened?

Dina: David went into the doctor's office while I sat in the waiting area. He was in there quite some time. He then came out and said to me that we were ready to go.

Rosie: Go? You did not get a chance to talk to the

doctor together.

Dina: Rose, we left the doctor's office and David did not speak to me.

Rosie: No, that's impossible.

Dina: It's true. It really happened.

Rosie: You will have to help me a little more. Probably you don't remember. You were in shock. Dina you know that I have talked to you about driving from that doctor's office in total anguish and despair. He must have said something.

Dina: No Rose, it happened as I told you.

Rosie: OK let's retrace your steps. You are in the car with David. He is about to start up the car. What did he say to you? What do you say to him?

Dina: I tried to ask him if he had anything to tell me and he abruptly said 'no.'

Rosie: What about when you reached traffic lights? No conversation?

Dina: Rose you don't understand. He did not speak at all except to say 'no' and that was it. What is even worse is that until the day he died we did not have a serious discussion about any of this.

Rosie: Dina you must be hiding something from me. It seems impossible for me to believe that.

Dina: Rose, you have to understand David's history. He did not speak a lot normally so now that he was in trouble he clammed up even tighter. He went into complete denial about his illness. He made new suits because he had lost so much weight, he actually moved into new offices like nothing new had occurred. The only obvious difference in his routine was that he sometimes came home a little earlier during the day and slept a little longer.

Rosie: I am trying to wrap my mind around these thoughts and I am having great difficulty.

Dina: There was one time I asked my husband if he gave a moment's thought to my feelings about being infected with HIV. He actually said that he did not know how to feel because probably it was me who had infected him by working at the lab at the university. How does anyone know who infected who.

Rosie: You know Dina that I think that most things can be forgiven but I think this is not one of them.

Dina: You know God has helped me to be here at this time. He has given me the strength to withstand all of this. I know that David knew that what he was saying was not true. There are worse things that came directly from his refusal to handle his HIV status.

Rosie: What could that be?

Dina: When he got really ill I always hired a nurse to stay with him if I had to leave the house. On my return the nurses would tell me what a wonderful husband I had, how he thanked them for their services. But he never thanked me once, not once – that was very painful.

Rosie: Let's talk about your grandchildren.

Dina: Yes, Paul and Melissa, they love their Grammy and I feel so fortunate to be in their lives and have a chance to love them back. But to continue on painful subjects, this is going to be the last painful subject that I will attempt to share with you. I am doing this because I want people to know that with God's help you can get through anything.

Rosie: It concerns Paul and Melissa, does it not?

Dina: Yes. When they were younger and I was left in the house with them, Sharon and I came up with a plan to protect the children from me in case I had a fall or a stroke and got cut. We had to teach them that in case Grammy fell they were not to touch Grammy. I don't know if you can imagine Rose what's that like, you have to tell your own grandchildren not to touch you. That was painful but that is what HIV/AIDS can do to families.

Rosie: Thank you very much, Dina.

Sadly I have put off writing this book so many times that Dina did not live to see this written account of how she managed HIV/AIDS. She got sick while visiting her family in Tulsa and had to be hospitalized there. Her grandchildren were so traumatized by this event they refused to open their Christmas gifts until Grammy was home. There could be no Christmas without their beloved Grammy. Dina returned to Jamaica very unwell. Her son Sheldon devoted himself to her care. My friend Shelly, my sister Andrea and I visited as often as we could. Even when Dina was not communicating with me verbally she still showed me where the books she had brought for me were kept.

When Dina died in the late summer of 2003, I was not feeling very well myself. At the time it was hard for me to distinguish between grief and loss and my own physical discomfort. As friends and family gathered at her home to comfort Sharon and Sheldon, I was upstairs in her room trying to get some reassurance from just being there. Later in the evening Sharon came upstairs to show me some old photographs of her mother. There was young Dina in London at her college graduation, a smiling Dina with her fellow graduates from Nursing school, Dina on dates, Dina visiting museums and quite a few photographs of Dina and her parents in cities all over Europe. Sheldon joined us, and as the three of us enjoyed the photos of a young Dina and the promise they emanated, for a moment we were lost in our own thoughts.

Then Sharon voiced hers. 'When I look at these photographs and think about my lovely, talented, gentle, cultured and courageous mother I can't help but be so upset with my father. How dare he!'

'You know Rosie,' Sheldon said, 'Sharon and I, without collaborating, have completely forgotten our father's birthday, the day that he died, all the dates that are connected to him – they are just gone.'

'They are all erased from our memories, just like that,' Sharon said.

Over that six-year period (1997–2003), Dina and I developed a great friendship, and now that she is gone I am at a loss to describe how I feel. Our relationship was so central to my being that it is difficult to go on without our daily telephone calls or her dropping by just to bring me a mango or something she had baked.

I met Dorothy on the telephone through a doctor. I liked her even though I was not as close to her as I was to Dina. Neither was our relationship as long term.

Dorothy (1995)

My name is Dorothy and my husband's name is Errol. Up to two years ago we were what I considered a normal Jamaican couple. We are both in our thirties. Errol is a professional and his job involves a lot of travelling oversees. I am a small business entrepreneur and I have recently taken a course at a tertiary institution. My son has just turned two and I also have Errol's son, Julian, from a previous relationship, living with us. He is in high school.

I had no notion that my husband, Errol, was ill. He is a fair-skinned, nice-looking man that exercises regularly and he looks after himself very well. About a year and a half ago he asked me to accompany him to the doctor because he wanted to discuss something with me. I was a bit apprehensive as Errol looked like what one would term, 'the picture of health'.

We both went into the doctor's office and then Errol started to speak. He told me that he had gone for his annual check-up for insurance purposes for his job and that the test results showed that he was HIV positive. My brain refused to accept the possibility that my husband had caught the virus that causes AIDS. I started to feel dizzy, but Errol and the doctor continued to talk, unaware of my physical discomfort. Then I heard the word bisexual and I was overcome.

The next thing I was aware of was Errol holding me and the doctor trying to revive me. I had fainted dead away. As I came back to reality my first thought was for my baby, Ramon. I can't believe that this was happening to my baby. We had a long discussion that afternoon as to the steps that were to be taken immediately, some short-term objectives they said: I heard it through tears.

I was still breastfeeding my son, and I had to stop immediately as I could have been endangering Ramon's life. They told me that I should be tested that day and since Ramon was too young to be tested they would know how to help my son depending on my test results.

I went through the next couple of days in a daze. I completely blocked out everything and everyone except my son. I dealt with him exclusively . . . Errol probably thought that I was losing my mind. I prayed day and night for a negative result even though I thought my chances were slim. I rationalized that since Errol was away a lot, and he had done similar tests every year, and was HIV negative for the last three times, I was hoping that he had not infected Ramon or me.

Fortunately for my son and me, the test result was negative. I was overjoyed. I was HIV negative. I was advised to test every three months initially then six months and then annually. To date I have been tested many times with the same negative results and the best news is Ramon, my son, is healthy and I don't have to worry about him.

But what can I do about Errol. Did his bisexuality frighten or shock me? Yes it did, I never saw him as a bisexual man. Many years ago when he was travelling for his job I got an anonymous letter that included a picture of my husband with his arm around another man's shoulder. They were obviously posing for the picture and the puzzling thing was that they both had on underwear.

I showed the picture to Errol and he explained it away. I think I am an intelligent woman and I bought his explanation. There is probably a part of us that must rationalize for our physic protection. In any case, right now I have some more immediate and pressing problems that I have to deal with.

I have to deal with economic issues and this is tied in with questions about the family. Is Errol going to get sick? Can I look after him while parenting a young child and a teenager? Should I send the teenager back to his biological mother? Do I tell Julian that his father is HIV positive? If I tell Julian that information, is it then fair to separate him from his father?

Another worry of mine is that we don't own a house and I have never been able to understand why this is so. I have to talk seriously with Errol to ensure that we buy one so that the children and I will be able to exist if anything happens to him.

A very immediate concern is dealing with Errol's sexual appetite. He always had a healthy sexual drive but it seems that it has increased since getting HIV. On the other hand my desire for sex has greatly diminished, as I am deadly afraid of contracting the virus from him. Recently I told him that he must use two condoms at a time and he has refused to do this. We are having a very hard time with this. I really do not know what to do.

We have a far way to go, but when I look at Errol he seems so fit, he is hardly depressed, he is verbally upbeat. His mantra is 'a positive attitude goes a long way towards survival', and he is certainly doing everything he can to make this a possibility.

He has linked up with some programme oversees and is getting his triple-cocktail therapy free of cost and together with vitamin supplements and regular exercise he thinks he can live a very long time.

I spoke to Dorothy often during 1996. She was willing to talk to me because she knew I was HIV positive and she thought that I might offer some perspective on what that feels like.

She knew I had two children and had gone through the agonizing decision to tell them of my status. She had many questions, which she wanted help in answering. For my part I was happy to pass on any information about my experience with HIV/AIDS to someone if it would make the journey a little less daunting.

I sensed that even though she brought up and spoke at length about her husband's bisexuality, she was not at ease getting feedback from a virtual stranger about this. I was an ear and I listened without many comments. She felt a certain steadfast security in her relationship with Errol and had decided to accept him for what he was. It seemed that she had found a level of accommodation where she exercised some control, which she was happy with. She even joked about her husband's psychiatrist whom they sometimes consulted together – that he seemed a little too friendly with Errol and as a result they stopped seeing him.

Dorothy was very anxious about her stepson Julian. He was very high on her list of priorities. We discussed for hours the pros and cons of telling him now or later about his father's HIV-positive status. He was a teenager, and she was terrified of making the wrong decision. I told her that what was important was that her decision be well thought out. She should encourage Errol to talk to a trained counsellor or child psychologist as to the steps to take when disclosing something potentially life-altering to a child. I found that guidance and advice from trained personnel was the key ingredient in making the disclosure not as devastating as it could be for everyone. Also important in minimizing the impact of disclosure was leaving the avenue clear for the child to get follow-up counselling.

Another issue that made Errol hesitant about disclosure was that he was feeling so well and thought it unnecessary at this time to put his son through this ordeal. In the final analysis, I told Dorothy, the family as a unit (Errol and Dorothy) should be on the same page in relation to what was best for Julian. A complicating aspect was Julian's biological mother, what she should be told and when.

Dorothy was very candid when she talked about her sexual relations with her husband. She saw the bedroom as a battleground and she was becoming war-weary. Errol's incessant sexual demands were burdensome to her. They had long discussions about sex and sex was always the dominant theme when Dorothy and I talked. I suggested that she speak to her doctor about the use of two condoms, because I had read in a magazine article that it might be risky. I found out just how much she wanted to resolve this part of her life one day when she called me on the telephone.

'Hello Dorothy. How are you today?' I had recognized her voice immediately.
'I am a little stressed, but I suppose no more than usual.'
'Is there anything special that you want to talk to me about today?'
'No, not really, Ramon has a slight cold but I got some medicine for him. I think he will be better soon.'
'How is Errol doing – did he get back his test results?' I inquired.
'Oh, they are good – his T-cells and everything is fine, he is so lucky.'
'I don't know if you can call Errol lucky – remember

he has the virus,' I commented.

'You know what I mean, he is healthier than most and nothing shows on him. Sometimes I wish I could be as optimistic about the future as he is, but I suppose we both can't be depressed,' Dorothy mused.

'You are depressed, are you really? I thought you were feeling better about things in general.'

'Yes and no, some aspects of the whole HIV saga are becoming more familiar so I wear them better, but the battle in the bedroom still rages on.'

'You should talk to your doctor about this.'

She whispered, 'I don't think any doctor can solve this, but you might be able to help us.'

'Why are you whispering all of a sudden? What is it you think I can do to help?'

'I have to whisper – can't you hear me?'

'Yes, but barely. Is there someone else in the room? Is that why you are not speaking up?'

'No, but let me change the telephone; I'll go to the bedroom.'

A few moments passed.

'Hello Rosie, are you still there?'

'Yes, I am.'

'I want to ask you something but I am a little embarrassed?'

'You can't be embarrassed to ask me anything at this stage; we have shared so many intimate details of our lives. Come on, what is it?'

She paused for a second then I hear her take a deep breath and say 'Rosie will you have sex with my husband? It will help me out a lot.'

I start to laugh, a self-conscious laugh. It was laughter that would soon get beyond my control and I wouldn't be able to stop.

'Rosie, are you laughing at me?'

'I don't know exactly why I am laughing. I suppose I am a little uncomfortable. The irony and the sadness of this . . .' I continue to laugh.

'You are laughing at me, at us . . .' Dorothy said.

'You should know by now that I can laugh at serious issues and I must tell you that the idea that my first invitation in years should come from a woman asking me to have sex with her husband is irony beyond belief.'

'Rosie,' she pleaded, 'I am asking because it would help me out a lot.'

I thought about the many facets of HIV and the brutal way it was making its voice heard in this conversation 'Dorothy, did you think this through?'

'Yes Errol and I discussed this.'

'You mean Errol suggested it to you and you ran with it.'

'He said that since you are both HIV positive it would be safe.'

'Safe, Dorothy? What is safe about having sex with an infected person, how can it be safe?'

'Errol said you both would not have to use a condom because you're both infected.'

I tried to decide what to do. Should I feel personally insulted and just hang up the telephone or try to see some humour in this situation.

'Rosie, are you still there?'

'Surprisingly I am. I can't believe that you thought that you could ask a question like this to anyone including me.'

'I did not mean to offend you, but you told me that you did not have anyone.'

'You seem to have forgotten a tiny detail, I am HIV positive. But let us forget about me for a moment and focus on you. What would you get from this deal as a woman?'

'You don't realize how much pressure I am under from Errol.'

'And you solve this by introducing into your marriage another third party? What do know about me? How do you know that I won't create more problems than you can handle? '

'I know that you are older than us and attractive.'

'I think I am out of my depth. I do not understand. I am missing a piece of the puzzle so I am unable to put the whole of the picture together.'

'Errol said . . .'

'I have a very important message for you to pass on to Errol. Dorothy, are you listening?'

'You are upset and I did not know that you would let a small thing like this upset you.'

'This is not a trivial matter, you have asked me, a stranger, to have sex with your husband. Your life has been turned upside down and I believe that you are inviting more crises into your life unnecessarily. I am not as upset as you think because if I were I would have been off this phone at least ten minutes ago.'

'How can you say that you are not upset when you are almost shouting?'

'I am so sorry. Please tell Errol that he has to use a condom every time he has sex.'

'But if both people are HIV positive it should not matter . . .'

'I remember that the doctor told my husband and me that if we were going to have sex we should use condoms. Listen to me and then ask your doctor. Remember that we have a test that we measure viral load. This means you can get more or less of the virus. Also they are different strains of the virus and he does not want to complicate his viral load.'

'Rosie, I have to go now. I'm so tired and I know you must be too.'

'I am sorry that this has to end on this note, but please remember to share with your husband all the things I have said.'

After my conversation with Dorothy, I was deeply disturbed by the implications of what she was going through at that time. I hoped that this phase of her HIV experience would be short lived.

When HIV and AIDS enter our lives there is the sudden jolt of its impact, followed by lingering doubts about our sexuality. Gradually the many tentacles of the virus intrude in every area of our existence. I believe we need to be vigilant and seek help from people with knowledge, or call on one's personal source or sources of strength and wisdom. The alternative is that the tentacles of HIV over our lifetime will strangle us.

Megan

Megan and I became friends just a short time before she immigrated to the United States. In the latter part of 1998 we were having supper together in an attempt to catch up on all the news of our lives.

'Rose, I have something to tell you. Michael has got himself into trouble. Think of the worst thing that can happen to him.'

'Megan, that's a little unfair I do not know him very well, I just know him through you. What is it? Tell me something to go on. I do not want to be guessing.'

'You will have to try.'

'You can't be insulted at anything I guess, all right?

'No, no, you go ahead.'

'Here goes, he has mishandled some money and is going to jail.'

'No, try again.'

'He is having an affair,'

'Something like that.'

'Megan, please tell me that he did not contract the virus.'

'Oh yes, he did. And I have been so angry that all the anger is gone. Now I just cry all the time.' Tears rolled down Megan's face as I hugged and comforted her.

'Wait a minute now, have you been tested?"

'Yes, quite a few times and up to now I am negative. You cannot imagine how badly Michael handled the whole situation. It could not be worse. He was inept and he put me at much greater risk than was necessary.'

'I don't mean to be a wet blanket, but have you given any thought to the fact that you might become positive?' My voice crackled. I tried to stop the tears but they were relentless now. Megan held both my hands in hers as she stretched across the table.

'Actually Rose, there is none. If I ever become HIV positive I will die. I will kill Michael or I will die because

I am not taking all those drugs, I cannot and will not put those drugs in my body. In either case I am a goner. I am not like you. I do not have the physical and emotional strength to take the hundreds of pills you take.'

'I do not take "hundreds", just a couple dozen and only half of that amount is my triple therapy. That might change. There are new drugs on the market everyday, and one a day might be a reality for some HIV-infected persons.'

'You talk about the medication like it's a cake walk but it has been terrible for you.'

'I agree, it is one of the many aspects of the disease that I struggle with the most. I don't know which is worse, the act of swallowing those many pills or the cost of the medication. I cannot get over the fact that I am literally ingesting Timothy's college education.'

'Please don't put it like that. I am sure everyone wants you to take the medication so that you will be around a long time.' There were more tears from Megan.

'In 1992 before I started taking the newer drugs I was taking AZT, and my friend Norma talked to me on the phone for one straight hour encouraging me to take the first pill. And just last year my sisters, Rena and Andrea, and my brother-in-law, Len stood vigil around my bed so that I would take the "hundreds" of pills you talk about.'

'I know that I cannot manage HIV. It would be a death sentence for me.'

'Speaking of death sentences – how is Michael? How are his tests? How is he feeling?'

'To tell you the truth, I really do not know and I am

not all that interested. I have just gone away. I have just unplugged from the whole situation. I can't sleep I can barely respond to people when they talk to me. I have told two friends, but I need details and they are not forthcoming from Michael. All I have are these turbulent emotions that I keep bottled up and I cannot speak to him.' She dabbed unsuccessfully to dry her tears.

'You know Megan, that even before HIV, I have been a strong supporter of managing one's mental health – you have to begin to think about it. It is dangerous to ignore the need for help. Michael needs help too. How are the children taking it? It must be hard on them.'

'Michael . . . Children . . . seeking help . . . that is not a part of Michael's HIV vocabulary.'

'This is crazy! Talk to me Megan.'

'He has closed me down. I am not allowed to tell anyone, least of all the children. He has no intention of telling anyone, not his family, not mine. His friends are in the dark.'

'How do you feel about his pronouncements?'

'Well . . . they are his. The children and I do not have a voice. He is concerned about his own squeaky image at the expense of all of us. Mister Nice Guy, Mister Goody Two-Shoes that's Michael my husband.'

'Megan, you have to help Michael and you can't help him by malicing him.'

'You are the only person I know on God's good earth that is capable of a response like this. Michael has committed adultery and he has contracted the virus that causes AIDS. By this one act he has changed all of our lives. He is sick and miserable now and he will remain like this all the rest of his life. The children are in a tension-filled house and they have no idea why their parents are responding to each in such negative ways. I did nothing wrong and I essentially have no husband. Now I must help him? He has to figure it out, especially because he has chosen to exclude me entirely from any serious discussion about how he got infected.'

'Please remember that I have a seven-year headstart in terms of HIV experience so I not only see the broader picture, I have lived it. I know this is relatively new to both you and Michael but you have to see the need for some sort of plan to make life a little easier for all of you.'

'New to me but not to Michael, I am so pissed he knew for sometime and just kept it to his goddamned self.'

'Do you know the specific length of time?'

'You are not listening to me Rose. He has refused to discuss anything with me, so specific knowledge I do not have and it is maddening to have to say that out loud.'

'Can I dare to say the word . . . sex?'

'What about sex – your favourite topic?'

'It's not my favourite topic, but we disagree on its relative importance inside a marriage. I believe that it's very important you don't.'

'You win.'

'I win what Megan?'

'Michael agrees with you. He says it is my lack of interest in sex that led directly to his getting infected with HIV. He blames me for everything.'

'You know intellectually that you are not responsible for Michael's behaviour. He should be a man and accept his getting the virus as a terrible mistake, and then he would be better equipped to accept and deal with all the ramifications of HIV infection. I hope you are not taking Michael's "lame blame" scenario very seriously. Emotionally this can be devastating for you.'

'My emotional state is so chaotic and possibly my only truth is that I know the source of all my woes is Michael. I sound pathetic. I know I should be packing and I am not. I can't even go there in my fantasy world without Michael. The only way I can explain it to myself is that economically we cannot afford to be apart.'

'But what about your sex life . . .?'

'Sex life . . . that is dead, which is a blessing in disguise because I can live without it.'

'You are a married woman and you are giving up sex in your early forties. The concept is truly daunting for me as your friend. HIV cannot affect us both the same way. My husband is dead, yours is not.'

'He might as well be – there is no way I am going there with Michael. The only sensible thing he has done is not to ask and not to give me any signs that he expects anything. The HIV apart, he betrayed me in the most fundamental way. I think the least a wife can expect from her husband is that he protects her, does not put her in danger. He knew that he was infected and did not tell me.'

'Did you two have unprotected sex after Michael was informed of his status?'

'I am not sure. He says we did not. There were a couple of times when we did use a condom. What is upsetting about that is that no alarm bells went off. What kind of woman am I that I did not notice that we were using condoms for the first time in ten years? I do not remember his explanation, some nonsense but I was not paying attention.'

'Don't be too hard on yourself. The "what if?" the "why me?" and the "how could I have missed it?" – many other women, including me have laid claim to all the self-recriminations that are possible. You Megan, on the other hand have something to be thankful for. You are not infected and we have to hope that it will remain so forever. What is your best guess as to the amount of time Michael knew before you did? Would it be about six months?'

'That would be as good a guess as any, I suppose.'

'So my dear friend, you are telling me with a straight face that in six months you had sex twice.'

'It might have been once . . . but don't you blame me.'

'I am not in any position to assign blame but I am so unhappy for you. You have had one sexual partner in your entire life and that is Michael, your husband. He has not been able to help you enjoy sex.'

'This is not the end of the world.'

'No, it is not, but you could have enjoyed your marriage a little more.'

'And I might have ended up HIV positive.'

'Your point is well taken Megan; you believe that your lack of interest in sex might have saved you from contracting the virus from Michael.'

'It just might have helped me personally but as long as that asshole Michael is infected we are all in the pickle together.'

'I want details about when you first heard about Michael. We definitely have to talk again. In the interim please promise me that you will think about, first of all, going to a counsellor and second, come up with some strategies that will make your life a little more palatable.'

'I can't promise you anything. I just do not think I can do a lot to make things better. I can tell you about the day my life was damaged beyond repair. Before I begin, tell me something that I am curious about. You always claim that you are able to read body language; did you ever guess that I would have this catastrophic news to share with you today?'

'I had absolutely no idea. You have to admit that HIV has many faces. They are hard to decipher.'

As Megan continued to share her account of Michael's deception with me, despair and helplessness flooded my being. It was two years later in the year 2000, that I discussed with Megan the idea of recording our pain and experiences with HIV/AIDS. I was particularly interested in the initial impact of the revelation of HIV infection. Megan emailed this account to be included in the manuscript.

Megan's Account (2000)

I remember that day as if it were yesterday. It started out, as being a typical Friday morning in January 1997 in anticipation of a well-deserved long weekend with Monday, Martin Luther King Jr's holiday. I hold a senior position in the human resource unit of a large corporation. We had just completed a major project. I was anxiously waiting for five o'clock to come in order to start this totally relaxing long weekend with no agenda to follow.

Well, little did I know that a phone call would put an abrupt end to all plans for the weekend and change my 'well scripted', outlined path that I envisioned my so-called life to be.

Here I am married to Michael, a real estate agent, for over 20 years. We both are from Jamaica and have lived in Orlando for ten years. We have two young adult children attending college. As a family we are going through the usual and the unusual growing pains, problems and heartaches involved in raising children. The telephone rang, 'Hello, this is Megan speaking how may I help you?'

'I am calling from Dr Franco's office; please hold a moment for Dr Franco.'

'Hello Mrs Simpson, how are you doing?'

'Good. . . . Thanks for asking.'

'I need to see you in my office today, anytime that is convenient to you, maybe after work hours.'

'Why, Dr Franco?'

'I would prefer to speak to you in person and it has to be today.'

'OK, I will call you back and let you know when I can make it.'

'That's not necessary Mrs Simpson you do not need to call me back, I will be here waiting on you. Goodbye. I will see you later.'

What the hell just happened? It is 1:00 p.m. and this stupid doctor says he needs to see me in his office today. Whatever he wants to see me about cannot be discussed over the phone. What does he mean? Discuss what? I have not been to the doctor for at least six months. What in the world could he want to see me about? Well, here I am waiting again for 5 o'clock to come for a totally different reason. The suspense is too much and I don't think I can wait. I have to come up with an excuse to tell my boss and get permission to leave office for a couple of hours.

I called Michael, my husband, and told him about the creepy phone call from the doctor. He said he would meet me at the doctor's office if I got the ok to leave.

Well I, being me, always scared of telling lies when it comes to illness, told my boss the truth, that my doctor called and wanted to see me in his office today. He told me I should leave right away. I called Michael and left the office at about 1:10 p.m. Michael was waiting for me in the parking lot of the doctor's office. 'Michael, what do you think this is all about? I am going to be so mad if this is something he could speak to me about over the phone.'

Michael accompanied me all the way to the doctor's office. I signed in at the reception area and waited for about 20 minutes. The nurse opened the door and called my name. Just as I got up to go into the doctor's office, Michael said he needed to speak to me outside for a minute.

'Michael, the doctor has called me inside his office I need to go in.'

'But there is something I need to say to you before you go in. I know what the doctor is going to tell you.' By this time Michael was hugging me close to him and would not let me go.

'Michael this is crazy, let me go.'(Laughing and feeling embarrassed that the doctor was waiting on me.) The nurse's voice intruded.

'Mrs Simpson, the doctor can see you now, he is waiting.'

Michael addressed the nurse. 'Can you wait a minute please, she will come in shortly.'

Michael took me outside the doctor's office and told me that he had had a blood test done recently and the doctor found something wrong. I started laughing. 'You are kidding, right? Stop this stupid thing. Let me go inside and see the doctor.'

'Megan, they found . . . ah.' Still he was hugging me closely. 'I am positive and I am so sorry.'

'Michael, please let me go for a minute so I can speak.' I could not speak because my mouth was buried in his shoulder. He was holding me so tightly. I started struggling to be released. After a while he let me go.

'Michael, what are you saying?'

'I am sorry, I am sorry, I am so sorry,' he kept on repeating.

'Anyway Michael, I am going back inside now because the doctor is waiting on me.'

When we entered the reception area again the nurse was still waiting at the door for me. Michael asked her if he could accompany me inside to see the doctor. The nurse, without hesitating, and in a stern voice answered, 'No, just Mrs Simpson.'

The nurse showed me in to the empty doctor's office and asked me to wait for a few minutes, as the doctor was finishing up with his last patient. Last patient? Who am I? Am I not a patient? I was sitting and thinking how rude the nurse was. She actually shouted and was rude to Michael. I had a few minutes to myself to try to comprehend and put in perspective the events that took place today that prompted my sitting here in the doctor's office. *It's now 2:30 p.m. The doctor called minutes to one. I called Michael. I asked my boss to leave early. Michael met me in the parking lot of the doctor's office. We went into the waiting area. The nurse called my name. Everything else is a blur. And now I am sitting here waiting. Doctor Franco came in, shook my hand and sat down. The nurse came in and stood by the doctor's desk.*

'Mrs Simpson, I have some disturbing news for you. Several months ago your husband came in with a letter from an insurance office stating that he was turned down for insurance because of some inconclusive blood test results. He was instructed to consult his physician. We ran a blood test that tested for HIV. The test results were positive.'

I was thinking to myself, *positive, positive*, where had I heard that word recently? Oh yes, Michael said he was positive. The doctor continued.

'I told your husband that he needed to inform you and that you should be tested too. I called him several times for many weeks to inquire if he had told you. I gave up after three months and called Tallahassee for information on the legal ramifications concerning doctor–patient confidentiality. I wanted to find out if I had the authority as your doctor to tell you of your husband's terminal illness. Mrs. Simpson I also need you to be tested today and I'll rush the processing so you will have the results as soon as possible.'

Speechless, motionless, stunned, scared, I must have sat there with no visible emotions, because the doctor said to me, 'Mrs Simpson, do you understand what I just said?'

'Yes Doctor, are you going to do the test today?'

I could not think of anything else to say. The nurse then turned to the doctor and said, 'Would you believe that Mr Simpson turned up with Mrs Simpson?'

I was too terrified to comprehend what she meant by that statement to the doctor. I went with the nurse and she took the blood to be tested. The doctor was waiting again for me in his office when I returned.

'Mrs Simpson, do you know how this disease is contracted?'

'Yes doctor, I know.' Still in shock, words were failing me now. 'But when will I get the results?'

'I will try to get it on Monday afternoon and you will have to come in again to the office to get the results.'

'OK, thanks very much, I am off on Monday so I will come in at 2:00 p.m. if that is convenient for you.' It was still very difficult for me to speak.

'Yes 2:00 p.m. is fine, but, Mrs Simpson, this situation that your husband has put you in is a very dangerous one. You have to protect yourself now. Whatever the results are, you still need to be careful and take the proper precautions to ensure that you will be protected. By my diagnosis and expertise your husband has had this disease for about 18 months now.'

I interrupted the doctor.

'I just remembered something. I did a HIV test to purchase insurance for a house we bought recently.'

'Yes Mrs Simpson your husband told me, but you need to get tested every three months for at least three years. I am hoping and praying that your results will be negative.'

'Anyway Doctor, I have to get back to work now. I told my boss that you asked me to come in today. What can I tell him now? I certainly do not want to tell him about this. Can you think of something else?'

'Mrs Simpson you can tell your boss that your potassium level was alarmingly high and I needed to see you to perform another test.'

'Thank you Doctor, I will see you on Monday.'

Michael was waiting for me in the reception area and hugged me again and again and said he was sorry. I just could not find the words to say anything to him. We walked down the corridor to the elevator and to the parking lot in total silence. He asked then if I was OK to drive back to work. I nodded and drove off.

A million questions were racing through my mind but the one that was most pressing was, *why me, why me, why me?* Everything around me seemed strange and unfamiliar as I drove back to work. I felt total hopelessness. *What is going to happen now? How must I deal with this new development? This has to be a dream. I am having the worse nightmare ever. I need to wake up now and everything will be back to normal.* As these thoughts swirl around my mind, I wonder if 'normal' will ever be in my life again. It is now 4:00 p.m. with only an hour to go before the weekend. I now need this weekend to end as quickly as it starts. I am not able to bear the suspense. *I need to know now.*

As I sat at my desk staring blankly at my computer screen and the clock simultaneously, everything around me seemed to be slowing down. *I want to – I must get out of here. The walls are closing in on me.* Suddenly I feel claustrophobic. I need air. I cannot breathe properly.

'Megan, are you all right?' a co-worker asked, while gently touching my shoulder.

'Ah, yes,' I answered, gulping down a cup of water that had been sitting on my desk since this morning.

Six years later, Megan is still HIV negative and the state of her marriage to Michael is essentially the same.

EVERY FOWL FEED PON 'IM OWN CRAW

In the crisis of life it's every man for himself

TWO STRANGERS CAME TO VISIT ME when I was ill in 1997 and directed me to Dr Steinhart in Florida.

I got to know Mr Smith and Mr Robinson very well. They introduced me to Dina later that year. They were both supportive of Dina and me. When Mr Smith attended conferences and received papers on alternative medical paths he would always ensure that I received copies. When my doctors could find no medical reason for the times when I fainted publicly, it was Mr Robinson who gave me a pamphlet on panic attacks and suggested that this might explain them. The knowledge gained from reading the pamphlet ensured that I never fainted publicly again. Mr Smith told me that he and Mr Robinson would purchase medication in bulk from overseas and would therefore be able to supply Dina and me with Zerit and Epivir at a reduced cost. Mr Robinson delivered the medication to us every month, so each month both Dina and I would write out cheques payable to him.

Over the years I became close to, and fond of Mr Robinson. When I noticed that he looked tired and had lost weight we spoke about this and he promised me he would rest some more, and try to reduce the stress in his life. In the summer of 2000 when my medication was not delivered, I tried to contact him at work and was told that he was off because of illness. His answering machine at home alerted me to the fact that he was staying with his mother. Alarm bells rang in my head: I thought about how he had looked and sounded the last time I saw him. When I spoke to him by telephone, he confirmed that he was gravely ill and had spoken to Dr Steinhart who he had not visited for over two years but who now prescribed medication for him.

I told Dina and she visited him that same day. My friend Carmen also volunteered to visit Mr Robinson for me, as I was not feeling well. She made vegetable soup and prepared natural fruit juices for him. Both Dina and Carmen reported to me that Mr Robinson did not look as bad as I had told them to expect. They thought that he would survive this particular bout of illness. I called Mr Smith to help quiet my trepidation. He told me that everything was under control. I offered a natural based topical cream that I thought would help Mr Robinson, but Mr Smith bluntly refused. I sent the cream anyway. I visited Mr Robinson a few days later. As I sat in the living room and he walked towards me I was reminded of the 'special walk' that very sick people have. My apprehension grew as we sat beside each other and talked.

'Mrs Stone thanks for the cream you sent for me, it helped a lot.'

'How are you feeling today?'

'I am not sure how to answer that. My appetite is gone and, ah, because my mouth is so badly infected I have to drink those protein shakes over there.'

'What medication did Dr Steinhart prescribe?'

'Here they are, I have to take one now.' He took out the capsule and tried unsuccessfully to break it in two. 'Mrs Stone, I am so weak, I can't even do this, and I have to put the contents in a shake, that's how I take it, can you help me?' He handed the capsule to me.

'Mr Robinson, I just look stronger, I am not sure that I am, but let me try.' My attempts to open the capsule were just as futile as his.

'I'll probably have to use a knife. Let me go and get it.' As he walked away from me, his gait looked more impaired than I imagined. My heartbeat quickened. He returned and drank the shake that contained the medication. 'Mrs Stone I have two things to talk to you about.'

'Yes, but are you sure you want to talk about this now?'

'You have to make sure that you never stop taking your medication.'

'You stopped taking your medication Mr Robinson, how come?'

'Mrs Stone, to tell you the truth I didn't have the money. What they are paying me barely covers expenses. So there is none left for any extra.'

'Why didn't you talk to Mr Smith about this? Couldn't he help?'

At this time I handed him my cash payment for that month's medication. He was too sick to go to the bank to cash a cheque. He took it from me and placed it beside my handbag.

'Mrs. Stone, this is something that you have to forgive me for, but it is not entirely my fault. I feel badly about taking this cash from you, but how my pay structure was set up was that getting money from you would be part of my pay. It is not that I think that you are rich or anything and can afford it but, I had to take payment from you as part of my salary.'

As I felt tears forming, he said, 'Mrs Stone, don't cry, forgive me.' He walked me to the door. As I reached my car, sobs rocked my body. I thought about the implications about what Mr Robinson had told me and the many months of $13,000 that could have gone towards feeding my children. HIV had again blindsided me. Trying to surviving HIV had allowed Mr Smith and Mr Robinson to go on a path outside of their normal character. Now Mr Robinson's economic distress could lead to him losing his life. It did. He died two weeks later.

A year later I was able to participate in an AIDS fundraising walk with my sister Rena in Florida, a physical triumph for me. I dedicated my effort to Mr Robinson and as I walked I told Rena all the good memories that I had of him, and how I wished my friend was still here with us.

EPILOGUE:
RAIN AND DARK CAN MEK
BARGAIN BUT DEM STILL CYAAN
BEAT SUN

Even when more than one bad circumstance oppresses you, you can look ahead to a brighter tomorrow

THE YEAR 2006 IS HALFWAY through and I am still alive. When Carl died in February 1993, I believed that I had only two years to live. I talked incessantly about dying with John, Norma and Shelly. I stopped buying clothes and looking in the mirror. I stopped watching television and reading for two years. In fact, I slowly lost interest in life. The positive that helped me to have any desire to participate was my children. I knew I had to interact with them, impart knowledge and experience and try to be present in their lives.

When I did not die, in my mind I started to extend my life one year at a time.

My friends intervened in this process and I started taking alternative medicine in order to maintain my health and to avoid illnesses that would compromise my immune system further. Despite my efforts, I became ill in mid-1997. Strangely, I now know that during the crisis period of my illness when some family and friends believed that I might die, I had no such premonition. It seemed that my certainty about impending death was inversely related to my state of health; when I was feeling well, I was sure I was dying but the minute that I became ill, I was sure that I would make it.

It was in Dr Steinhart's office during this period that

I made a conscious decision to stay alive. It would have been easier both financially and physically to choose death. My viral load was in the thousands (as opposed to undetectable); my T-cell count was two (instead of between 800 and 1,000). It took a herculean effort, on my part, to choose to take the triple-therapy route and to stay on course. For the next seven years, Viracept, Epivir and Zerrit became my constant companions along with a host of support medication. When I could no longer afford Viracept, Viramune was substituted. Apart from the havoc the medication wreaks on you internally, there are external manifestations of taking such toxic medication for an extended period (nine years).

My body weight and shape changed often. It was not just a matter of getting slim or putting on weight. It was that individual body parts were reshaped. From my diagnosis in 1992 to the present (14 years) my dress size has fluctuated between six and sixteen. In 2004, fat displacement became a part of my life. I was diagnosed with having lipodystrophy, a side effect of the medication. Dr Steinhart explained to me that sometimes when the medication is working well, lipodystrophy is a resulting condition. Essentially, fat moved from my arms and legs so they became thin. In addition to this the veins in these areas began to protrude and became very visible. The fat was then stored in the abdominal region, around the jaw line and under the chin. When I look in the mirror, I do not recognize the person looking back at me.

Some doctors believe that Zerit is most responsible for this displacement of fat. Earlier this year, Dr

Steinhart suggested that I come off of Zerit to help alleviate the problem. I was put on Combivair, which is a combination of Epivir and AZT. My triple therapy now consists of Viramune and Combivair. In 1997 I took 13 tablets daily for my triple therapy; in 2006 I take only four tablets daily.

The medication is now widely available in Jamaica and my cocktail can now cost me as little as J$2,000 per month, a far cry from the J$40,000 (US$1,500) per month that I was paying in 1997. Drugs are now available free of cost to the people who cannot afford it, through the Clinton initiative and other such efforts. The test for viral load is now available in Jamaica. Access to drugs and treatment has significantly improved here since 1992.

When I think of all the improvements in Jamaica, in terms of the array of treatment options, I am happy that all this has taken place. Yet I am also saddened because I know many people died in the past because they could not afford treatment, some of whom I knew.

I am still trying to understand why in 2006 Carl's mother and I are barely in contact. One of the constants for most of my 18-year marriage with Carl was a close relationship with her. I thought this relationship one of the better mother-in-law/daughter-in-law relationships that I had witnessed with friends and family. It was born out of the love we both had for Carl but it developed on the mutual respect we had for each other as women. In the 15 years that we were close, unless one or the other was off the island, Mother and I spoke by telephone at least twice per day. This relationship seemed natural, inevitable and not forced on either part. I did not discuss Carl or my relationship with him in any profound way with her, so I believed that our relationship existed on a level that was outside the realm of Carl's existence.

I enjoyed being in Mother's company as we performed routine activities together. I transported her to visit her friends and family, to Mammee Bay, to go shopping, to go to church, to her doctors' appointments, and I even accompanied her to funerals. Mother developed a friendship with my mother that evolved from their mutual Christian beliefs. My mom was part of a prayer partnership group at the Bethel Baptist Church, which welcomed Mother into the group during a particularly difficult health challenge in her life. This friendship with Mother extended to some other members of my large immediate family whom she felt free to call upon individually from time to time. They all liked Mother and developed their own relationships with her. One drawing card was that she liked baking, cooking and sharing with everyone who visited her. Mother even baked my wedding cake. Lisa, Norma and Shelly, three of my close friends then, all had relationships with Mother at various times.

Yet, my last conversation with Mother was nearly a year ago, in October 2005, when I called her to tell her of my mother's death.

Immediately after Carl's death when the relationship started to unravel, I tried to stop the deterioration by keeping Leroy abreast of various incidents that I am too embarrassed to write about now. These occurrences made me feel that I did not have the relationship that I thought I had with Mother, and sometimes that she did not like me at all. I had to conclude that our relationship did not exist outside of Carl. Leroy tried his best to mend the bridge between us. He even recorded a conversation with Mother that he played back to me – one in which he encouraged her to remember all the things that I had willingly done for and with her that neither he nor Carl were able or willing to do.

I appealed to Mrs Chamberlain, Mother's friend and former principal of Mona Prep School where my children once attended, to speak with Mother on my behalf. She assured me that Mother had never said anything negative about me to her. She suggested a meeting. I agreed. I was upset and disturbed to be meeting at Mother's house for this reason, so soon after Carl died. The meeting lasted an hour during which I spoke frankly of all the wrongs that I thought Mother had meted out to me. She told us that some of her actions might not be justified but she was just 'a little old lady, trying to cope with her son's death'. At the time, Dr Matt also agreed with Mother's explanation of her actions. I had difficulty then believing that grief could lead to a reversal of one's personality. I still have difficulty with this explanation.

I had gone as far as commissioning a painting from one of Jamaica's more prolific painters, David Pottinger, to capture the essence of Mother's and my wonderful relationship. It is now a standing joke with my friends and family members that I thought our bond was like that of the bible's Ruth and Naomi: 'and Ruth said: "entreat me not to leave thee, or to return from following after thee; for whither thou goest, I will go; and where thou lodgest, I will lodge.'" (Ruth 1:16).

The part that HIV/AIDS played in the breakdown of this relationship is difficult to assess. I was so hurt, disappointed and bewildered, that I did not share with Mother that Carl was dying of AIDS and that I was infected with the virus. I revealed this to her, finally, in 2000 and she expressed sadness and a willingness to assist me in any way she could. Yet the only time I see or hear from Mother now is when I initiate a visit or a call.

The loss of friendships has become part of my HIV landscape. Losing Lisa's friendship has been one of the saddest for me. I think that I have tried everything to mend the damage that was done when I did not tell her of my 'positive' status but told others. She felt I betrayed our friendship by allowing others to take the place that she should have had. This separation is directly related to how I handled my HIV status and the revelations afterwards.

Sharing my HIV status with family and friends removed the burden of lying, which had weighed on me for several years. Writing five articles anonymously for the *Gleaner* in 1995 under Father Tony's guidance sewed the seeds for the idea that I could and should share my story with a wider audience. I knew that I did not want to hide anymore but I had to think long and hard about how such a book would affect my family, especially my children. For me, the freedom to be able to speak openly about my HIV status to anyone I choose would be priceless.

One of the expectations of some of my friends and

family when I shared my HIV status with them was that I would feel the freedom to socialize more. It is hard to explain how the physical and social realities of HIV worked together to limit my world. Since being diagnosed, I have never felt entirely well. Interacting socially when I was feeling unwell was sometimes too much of a challenge. Added to this, there were specific bouts of illness. Though these bouts were not severe enough to send me to bed, they were difficult to handle away from home, and meant that whoever I went out with had to help. For example, the nausea and diarrhoea that resulted from my taking medication meant that I could go out only when these symptoms were at their mildest. I would have to be armed with medication for these two ailments plus my normal HIV medication cocktail. I would have to be assured that the toilet facilities would be close at hand. Whoever I went with had to be in eye-contact range, be familiar with my body language, pay close attention and be ready to help when I needed them. This limited whom I went out with to four people whom I trusted completely. After a couple of times I felt this responsibility was too burdensome for them and that it took the joy out of going out. As a result, since 1997 I went out less and less, and finally not at all.

My social world slowly shrank. I was now always at home and so had to build social relationships around staying at home. My extended family provided the base for this; my mother and father, my children Tricia and Timothy, my sister Andrea and my brother Barry. Visits from friends and other family members were and still are satisfying to me. The telephone, which I used a lot before I became ill, became my only direct contact with the outside world. I needed to find something to not only entertain me but make me feel a part of the world again.

My love of all sporting events drew me back to watching television again. Watching tennis, golf, cricket, football, the NFL, track and field events, and basketball are always highlights in my life. My nephew Maurice Wignall, a 110-metre hurdler, provided me with excitement and joy over his career. He being a finalist at the 2004 Olympics and a gold medal winner at the 2006 Commonwealth Games brought even more joy. The local broadcast on CVM and TVJ that carried the Caribbean feed of the Olympic games provided first-class coverage and commentary.

Venus and Serena Williamses' entry and their amassing of many major titles in tennis were just as enjoyable as the artistry and domination of Roger Federer's play and the recent ascendancy of James Blake's ranking. Tiger Wood's mastery of the game of golf ensured my viewing of all tournaments he has ever played. When there is an event like world cup football, the majors in golf and tennis, and the Olympics, I participate as if I were there and experience withdrawal symptoms when they end.

Along with sports, another must-see TV programme for me is Charlie Rose on PBS. Friends and family understand that during this broadcast period I am unavailable. Charlie Rose interviews people from all over the world, in all categories of life, from King Hussein of Jordan to Spike Lee, from literary prizewinners to Nobel prizewinners and I particularly enjoyed the one-hour interview with Magic Johnson. Charlie Rose's recent trip to India and his interviews there were most engaging. His love of movies ensured that I was able to see interesting conversations with all my favourite actors. Apart from being interested in the same topics and people as he is, I channel my love of travel through his interviews.

Reading widely was one of my favourite intellectual pursuits and hobbies. HIV and its physical manifestations interfered with this a great deal. When I was feeling well enough to read, my niece Kisha, who lives in Florida, provided me with appropriate reading material, which included a lot of books on Oprah's book club list. I thoroughly enjoyed my Christmas gift from her, which was Oprah's Twenty-Fifth Anniversary CD Collection.

Thirteen years ago at Carl's thanksgiving service I wondered if I would be around to be involved in the Carl Stone Memorial Scholarship Fund. Since then, nine young Jamaicans from the faculty of social sciences of the University of the West Indies have been awarded scholarships or bursaries to assist with their education. The Carl Stone Prize for Political Sociology which Carl gave to the best student in the class when he was alive, has been continued and has been upgraded by the scholarship fund.

In 1996 when I revealed to a friend that I was HIV positive, she told me that I should not have been afraid to tell people close to me because they all loved me and would do anything for me. She added, 'Not that I would drink out of the same glass with you.' That unpleasant remark was indicative of the fear and social stigma attached to HIV and AIDS at that time. But despite more awareness and information available, have people's attitudes really changed? Ten years later another friend refused to take me to a party with her. One reason given – she was afraid her family members would not want to drink out of the same glass with me.

In 2004, a male acquaintance of mine who usually calls me for cooking tips once asked me to bake a ham for him, which I did. He later confessed to me that he had a hard time eating the ham knowing that a person with HIV had prepared it. I had to remind him that he had a first degree in Physics and two masters degrees. He knew that his response was not related to any fact about HIV or AIDS but he still could not shake his apprehension about my baking the ham.

At a particular church in Jamaica, HIV-infected people came to share their stories with members of the congregation. At the end of the service, attendees were unsure if they should give these infected people lifts in their cars. They all wanted to help but were genuinely concerned for their safety. Though significant progress is being made in certain areas, we have a long way to go in eradicating the stereotypes and misinformation about HIV and AIDS.

I have been asked many questions: Did you know about Carl's infidelity? Did you yourself have an affair? How could you forgive him? Why did you stay with him? Do you have any idea of how you have managed this whole issue? How can you say that you had a happy marriage? The only question that I can answer definitively is that I did not have an affair. I am now reading *Stumbling on Happiness: 'Think You Know what*

Makes You Happy?' by Daniel Gilbert and I think I know why I cannot answer the other questions definitively. He speaks about us as 'having a *psychological immune system* that defends the mind against unhappiness in much the same way that the *physical immune system* defends the body against illnesses.' (162) He further states that, 'a *healthy* psychological system strikes a balance that allows us to feel good enough to cope with our situation but bad enough to do something about it.' (162) I hope that both my physical and psychological immune systems remain in some kind of balance to ensure a little more living.

Dr Richard has been treating me for the past four years. He has contributed significantly to my health and in him I have found a professional who is not only knowledgeable, but responsive to my particular needs. He always reminds me how important exercise is and that I should walk at least three times per week for half an hour. In this regard my friend Jennifer has walked with me for many years. Donna, my friend from university days who was one of the 20 guests at my wedding, provides me with much laughter. If laughter is the best medicine, she has provided me with large doses. Wanda, a nurse, who is a part of the circle of friends that included Lisa, has been a close friend and advocate. She registered and paid for me to participate in a course, sponsored by the Florida Department of Health, on HIV Prevention Counselling and Testing in 2004. I enjoyed both the academic and practical aspects of this course.

My granddaughter, Chloe Savannah-Rose, Tricia's daughter, was born two weeks before my mother died.

To the delight of my family, Mama was able to hold Chloe in her arms and we have a picture to mark the occasion. My 86-year-old father is enjoying his seventeenth great grandchild. Chloe is loved immeasurably by her grandaunts and granduncles. Timothy adores his niece. On a personal level, my granddaughter filled a void created by my decision not to touch other people's babies. The infusion of happiness that her presence brings is the perfect counterbalance to the challenges of my life's journey. I am saddened by the fact that Carl is not here to share in this joy.

BAXTER'S MOUNTAIN

MANDEVILLE TEACHERS' COLLEGE opened its doors to students in 1965. I was among the second batch of students who went there to get a Teacher's Diploma. This involved two years residential academic training and one year practical internship teaching at a school.

When I arrived at college we were told that our accommodation on campus was not ready. We could see work being done frantically on Jones and Kerr-Jarrett Halls. Some of us were paired together and slept in homes in and around Mandeville. 'Friends of Mandeville Teachers' College' was the group that was responsible for housing us. After a couple of weeks, the rest of the student body arrived and we were told that we would have to sleep at Moorlands Camp which was a few miles outside Mandeville. We were installed there for the first semester. Some students endured, others enjoyed their time at the Camp and the adventure of travelling to and from campus daily.

We were told that our college was involved in an experimental plan to reopen 'closed' schools. These were schools that were closed because the Ministry of Education did not have the staff to man them. The schools were usually located in remote areas in Jamaica that were sometimes difficult to access. I do not know what motivated others to sign up (because this was voluntary) but I thought of it as an adventure; a way to get to know another part of the island and since I would not be at home in Kingston, this would mean more independence for me.

Towards the end of our second year, the parish, the school and the names of the four students who would be going to these remote schools were posted on the bulletin board. Some students were visibly upset; they could not find the names of towns on the Jamaican map. Baxter's Mountain was one of them.

As the four of us gathered our collective fear and excitement, we spoke to the lecturer responsible for this and she advised us that Baxter's Mountain was about five miles from Annotto Bay in the hills of St. Mary. This location was in the east of the island which was closer to Kingston than to Mandeville. Apart from the geographic challenge, we were going to be teaching students seven to twelve years old. We were all trained to teach in the secondary/high school system, that is, ages 12 to 17 years. While I had observed other students teaching at the kindergarten and primary levels, my own teaching practice was at Homewood High, teaching 16 year olds, and Christiana New Secondary, teaching 13 year olds.

We were not deterred by this new challenge. We were sure that our excellent training, our youthful exuberance plus the fact that we were doing something noble for our country, would help us to succeed.

We visited Baxter's Mountain in July 1968, a few months before our formal taking over of the school.

We stopped in Annotto Bay to ask directions for the school and soon found out that there were people who were expecting us. Nearly all the business folk along the main road were anxious to meet us.

We drove about four and a half miles along a road that was asphalted for only half a mile. We hardly saw any houses because it seemed as if we were driving through the middle of sugar cane plantations on the right and banana fields on the left. Fort George was the name of the next small town that we encountered. It consisted of two small shops with a car parked at one of these shops. We did not know at the time but that car was to become very important to us.

Mr Clarke, the owner of the car, told us we were to go another mile and a half across the river to get to Baxter's Mountain. It was then that I noticed the river; it was just there, meandering, without a bridge. At that point I asked, 'What happens if we come here without a car that can go across this river? How do people normally get across?'

'Oh, Miss, yu jus' tek off yuh shoes and walk carefully on de smoode stones and enjoy de wata. An wen yu reach cross, yu mus' 'ave someting fi wipe yuh foot wid.'

'Really?' Val said in her quiet melodic voice.

'An miss, yu have fi watch de riva, if it is higher dan dis, yu caan cross.'

As we crossed the bridgeless river, we were quiet, as the terrain had become more mountainous and the road very narrow and winding. When we saw the teacher's cottage and the small building that was the school we all breathed a sigh of relief. It was not as bad as we thought. Student teachers from the pioneering class (first batch) had reported to us that when some of them arrived at their closed school they had to literally get machetes to chop their way through, to find a pathway just to get a glimpse of the school and the residence. Some places were almost uninhabitable. Those teachers survived and did excellent work for their pupils and also for the communities in which they found themselves.

I learnt a lot at Baxter's Mountain. With the Education Officers' help and a lot of reading material that was provided, I tried to master teaching techniques for the six to eight year old children that I taught at the school. We went to seminars twice a month on a Friday in Highgate, another town in St. Mary. These were beneficial to us not only because we learnt a lot from the seminars themselves, but there was also the interchange of ideas and experiences of other interns. And we got a chance to socialize with them. We also got visits from our tutors from the college which served to 'keep us on our toes' but they provided useful commentary on our class management and the quality of our teaching practices.

A few months after Carl died, in my anxiety to share with my children something that had meant a lot to me and give them an experience of another slice of Jamaica that was unfamiliar to them, I drove them to Baxter's Mountain Primary School. In my grief I did not think it through.

My stories were not age-appropriate and they did not take account of the trauma the children had gone through. I did not know that modernization had come to Baxter's Mountain. Most of my stories that involved the river would now seem unbelievable.

All four of us, Valarie, Marjorie, Phyllis and myself had a final paper to hand into the office in Highgate, towards the end of our internship programme in June of 1969. We had asked Mr Clarke to deliver them to the office for us. That evening, we walked down to Fort George, as we usually did, to give the four folders to him. As soon as we reached the river the rain started to come down in a slight drizzle. To protect our papers, we hid them under my blouse and I folded my arms around myself. The others linked their arms through mine as we slowly tried to navigate the crossing. We had just reached halfway across when we suddenly felt that the river had become stronger. We all became quiet as we held on to each other more tightly and used all our strength to reach the other side. We did not realize that it had been raining in the hills. We were grateful that our arms were linked and we had become one large unit instead of four smaller ones.

Another life-changing event involved a child in my class. The day I took a seven-year-old boy, Ramon, in my arms and walked to Mr Clarke, so that he could transport me to the nearest hospital in Annotto Bay, four miles away, I knew I had started to live, to experience, to know, to understand. I cleaned Ramon's nails with mine while we were in the waiting area of the hospital, and hoped that he would not vomit again or that no more worms would try to make their way out of his nostrils. I could feel my sense of virtue overwhelm me; now in my early twenties my patriotism was at its peak. Ramon was treated that day and was well enough to return to school in a couple of days.

One weekend, as Valerie and I got ready to leave Baxter's Mountain for Kingston, we noticed a medical personnel vehicle parked outside of the school gate. We asked for, and were offered a lift by the Annotto Bay Hospital van. While in the van, we realized that the doctor had come there to perform an autopsy on the corpse of an elderly woman. It seemed as if the autopsy was going to be performed at the school gate because four people had carried the body from deep in the hills to the school gate, as the van could not go beyond the school gate. The driver noticed that it had started raining in the hills, so the site of the autopsy was changed to the other side of the river, at Fort George. We drove down, over the river, the driver parked and waited while the four men brought the body to the riverside. By now the rain had started. The men laid the body on the banks of the river and moved away. From my vantage point, in the van, I could see when the doctor's assistant got out with his tools and opened the chest of the corpse. He then inserted his hand into the cavity, took out the heart and held it in his hands. He said to the doctor, 'See it yah, doctor.' The doctor, still in the van, looked through the window at the heart in the hand of his assistant and said, 'Ok, sew it up.'

I felt that the culmination of experiences in my internship year increased my knowledge storehouse one hundred fold. What seemed like everyday occurrences, and just part of life and living was, for me, a revelation. When I planned a school trip to Kingston, it was amazing to know that there were students in my class who had never been out to Annotto Bay, four miles away, much less to Kingston. I had to plead with some parents to send their children, and what was incredible about this was that the parents did not see this trip as a necessity, as part of the educational process. I observed and took part in the heart of interpersonal relationships among the teachers. I learnt how to arbitrate between students. Being at Baxter's Mountain Primary School made me realize that I loved teaching children, and that the entire process had become a part of how I defined myself.

IN MEMORIAM

While writing this manuscript seven people died whom I truly loved. I have included them because they have affected my life in profound ways.

Mark Bragg, 2002 – Died after a battle with cancer. His memory is alive in his widow Nicky, his children and grandchildren. I will always remember dancing with you, you did that so well.

Enid Edwards, 2003 – You were such a good person and a wonderful friend, I miss you a lot.

Winnifred Wignall, 2005 – My mother – I realized you had to go because your enlarged heart stopped working. You will remain in your family's individual and collective hearts. We hope that we can be a fraction of the friend, wife and mother you were.

Alvin Wignall, 2005 – My uncle – Your mind left before your body did. I remember the happy, jovial, full of jokes Uncle Alvin. Your family will always keep your memory alive in their heart.

Carlton Clarke, 2005 – Cancer took you too. We met as children on Phillip Road. Your knowledge of music was unmatched. I will never forget when my brother Mark asked you to play for Daddy's eightieth birthday. I thank you for the joy you gave to my parents.

Roy Johnson, 2006 – My cousin – You died at the hands of a gunman while you were trying to do a good deed for an older citizen. Thoughts of you will always remain with your family especially your children.

Diane Smart, 2006 – Cancer took you away too soon. Your home, along with your parents and your sisters were a central part of my early life. I remember with joy your last visit with me when you were accompanied by your sisters, Merris, Carol and Leonie.

AIDS FACT SHEET

Between January 1982 and December 31, 2005, 10,553 people had been reported with AIDS in Jamaica. Of these, 58 per cent are men and 42 per cent women. In total 6,341 people have died. Of these, 60.1 per cent were male and 39.9 per cent female.

HIV

Human Immunodeficiency Virus – HIV is a retrovirus. Retroviruses are capable of using an enzyme in the host cell to reproduce. Once HIV enters the human body, it targets and infects T-cells and eventually destroys them. Rather than being the direct cause of death, HIV sets up the body so that opportunistic infections or conditions can attack and cause damage. Once your body can no longer defend itself, even a common cold or influenza can be difficult for the body to get rid of. Over 25 opportunistic infections or conditions are associated with HIV/AIDS.

AIDS	Acquired Immuno Deficiency Syndrome – You have AIDS if you
	(1) test positive for HIV
	(2) have a T-cell count of less than 200* and
	(3) have been diagnosed with one or more opportunistic infections or conditions associated with AIDS.
Protease Inhibitors	These are considered one of the most powerful drugs against HIV. They are substances that interfere with viral protease which is an enzyme necessary for making viral protein, without which the virus cannot function.
T-Cells	(*Thymus Cells*) The cells in the body responsible for the defense of the immune system. T-cells are found in most body fluids, therefore HIV may be

---

* In July 2005, the AIDS case definition used for the Epidemiologic update, in Jamaica, was revised to include people with advance HIV (that is, people with T-cell counts of less than 350).

found in almost every human fluid. However, HIV has not been isolated in sweat, and the number of T-cells in fluids like saliva, urine and tears is minute, so these fluids do not transmit HIV. Blood, semen, vaginal secretions and breast milk contain high volumes of T-cells. These body fluids may transmit the virus through both sexual and blood-to-blood contact and through breastfeeding.

T-cell Count	Measures the amount of T-cells per cubic millimeter of blood. The T-cell count in a healthy adult is approximately 800–1,000.
Viral Load	A measure of the severity of a viral infection.
HIV Viral Load	The quantity of the HIV that is in the blood.

HIV can be transmitted through unprotected sex, via infected blood or from an infected pregnant woman to her unborn child. It is a very fragile virus that does not live outside the body for long and it certainly cannot penetrate unbroken skin.

For many years there have been mass publicity and education programmes designed to inform people how HIV is transmitted. In the early days there were mixed messages – some health campaigns led people to believe they should avoid practically all contact with an infected person. This led to people with HIV and AIDS being ostracized from society.

These days more is known about the virus and how it is transmitted. The most common method of transmission is though unprotected sexual intercourse with an infected person. HIV is found in vaginal and penile fluids which are produced before and during sex.

There are many urban myths surrounding how HIV is transmitted. You CANNOT get it from kissing, coughing or sneezing and certainly not from swimming pools, showers or toilets. It is not spread through mosquito bites and, provided an unbroken condom is used, it will not get through while having sex.

Basically HIV transmission requires very close contact with vaginal fluids, semen, breast milk or infected blood.

www.guide4living.com/hiv-aids/transmission.htm

BIBLIOGRAPHY

Allsopp, Richard. *A Book of Afric Caribbean Proverbs*. Kingston: Arawak Publications, 2004.

Anonymous, 'Protect Yourself', *Gleaner*, October 10, 1995.

———, 'The Pain of Discovery', *Gleaner*, October 19, 1995.

———, 'HIV Sufferer Battles for Life', *Gleaner*, October 27, 1995.

———, *Gleaner* Articles (various), November–December 1995.

Beckwith, Martha W. *Jamaican Proverbs*. New York: Vassar College, 1970.

Florida Department of Health. *HIV/AIDS 500*. 2001.

Gilbert, Daniel. *Stumbling on Happiness*. New York: Random House, 2006.

Ministry of Health. *National HIV/STI Control Programme. Facts and Figures, HIV/AIDS Epidemic Update*. Kingston: Government of Jamaica, 2005.

Stone, Rosemarie. *The Stone Columns: The Last Years Work*. Kingston: Sangster's Bookstore, 1994.

Walter, Ingrid and Sabina Theobalds. *A Sea of Wisdom: Island Proverbs*. Toronto: Walter and Co, 2004.

Zach, Paul. *Jamaica*. Singapore, Hong Kong: Apa Productions (HK) Ltd, 1983.